SEVENTH EDITION

Field Experience

A Guide to Reflective Teaching

George J. Posner

Cornell University

Craig Vivian

Monmouth College

Boston   Columbus   Indianapolis   New York   San Francisco   Upper Saddle River
Amsterdam   Cape Town   Dubai   London   Madrid   Milan   Munich   Paris   Montreal   Toronto
Delhi   Mexico City   Sao Paulo   Sydney   Hong Kong   Seoul   Singapore   Taipei   Tokyo

Vice President and Editor-in-Chief: Jeffery W. Johnston
Acquisitions Editor: Meredith D. Fossel
Editorial Assistant: Nancy Holstein
Vice President, Director of Sales and Marketing: Quinn Perkson
Marketing Manager: Darcy Betts Prybella
Marketing Coordinator: Brian Mounts
Senior Managing Editor: Pamela D. Bennett
Senior Operations Supervisor: Fran Russello
Cover Designer: Lisbeth Axell
Cover Art: Getty Images Inc.
Full-Service Project Management: Karpagam Jagadeesan,
    GGS Higher Education Resources, A Division of PreMedia Global, Inc.
Printer/Binder: Bind-Rite Graphics
Cover Printer: Phoenix Color Corp
Text Font: 10/12 Palatino

Credits and acknowledgments borrowed from other sources and reproduced, with permission, in this textbook appear on appropriate page within text.

Every effort has been made to provide accurate and current Internet information in this book. However, the Internet and information posted on it are constantly changing, so it is inevitable that some of the Internet addresses listed in this textbook will change.

Library of Congress Cataloging in Publication Data

Posner, George J.
  Field experience: a guide to reflective teaching / George Posner, Craig Vivian.—7th ed.
      p. cm.
  Includes bibliographical references and index.
  ISBN-13: 978-0-13-701687-7
  ISBN-10: 0-13-701687-5
  1. Student teaching.   2. Reflective teaching.   3. Teaching—Vocational guidance.   4. Teachers—Training of.
  I. Vivian, Craig T.   II. Title.
  LB2157.A3P6 2010
  370.71'1—dc22

2009011437

www.pearsonhighered.com

10 9 8
ISBN-13: 978-0-13-701687-7
ISBN-10:   0-13-701687-5

PREFACE

*F*ield Experience is intended to help students who are engaged in teaching-related fieldwork reflect on their experiences. Whether the students' field experiences consist of tutoring someone in biology, working with a reading group, leading a 4-H group, assisting an experienced English teacher with a whole class, or taking sole responsibility for teaching a social studies class, this book will help students learn from the experience. As such, it can be used as the primary text for early field experiences or student teaching or as a supplementary text in courses with field components, such as educational psychology, methods of teaching, and introduction to elementary or secondary education.

Topics include an examination of the students' concerns and goals regarding field experiences, the use of fieldwork logs, the study of the school and the community, observation of learners, interviews with the cooperating teacher, the analysis of lessons and curricula, an examination of one's own perspective on teaching, and the use of concepts from foundations and methods courses to facilitate reflection on teaching.

This book is designed to provoke thought; it is not a text filled with facts to memorize, nor is it a handbook filled with dos and don'ts. If it is to stimulate reflection, students will have to do more than read this book. They will have to respond to questions, do exercises, analyze experiences, and state personal beliefs. In order to encourage this type of active involvement, the book provides space for students to write down their responses. Some of these devices will provoke more thought than others and, therefore, require more extensive and detailed responses. Some will help students work out problems they are having, whereas others will seem irrelevant to their particular field experience. Students should feel free to focus their attention on the questions and exercises that seem most pertinent to their situations.

Although the entire book is intended for use throughout a teacher education program, certain chapters are more appropriate for certain phases of the program than others. Chapters 1 to 3 are orientation chapters and are most useful before placement in a field experience. These three chapters aid in the selection of the most appropriate positions and in the use of fieldwork logs for weekly reflection on field experiences. Chapters 4 to 11 are best used to help prepare for the field experience once the position is chosen and during the early weeks of the experience. Chapter 12 helps reflection on the field experience as it nears completion. The Epilogue at the end of Chapter 12 assumes the completion of the field experience and suggests ways of reflecting on it in order to prepare for the next experience. The appendixes provide actual examples of student fieldwork logs and progress reports as well as several self-assessment instruments.

The book's chapter organization is intended to provide flexibility of the text for use in elementary and secondary settings and in a wide range of subject-matter-specific courses. You are encouraged to use the text in whatever order is appropriate to your particular syllabus.

This new edition retains many of the features of the sixth edition, including the basic organization of chapters. The major additions consist of action research, diversity, and student teacher–cooperating teacher interactions.

ACKNOWLEDGMENTS

This book is in some ways a collage of ideas relevant to field experience in teaching. Although each chapter reveals the influence of many people and their writings, most chapters reflect the influence of one or two principal pieces of work.

The dominant influence on Chapter 1 was Joseph Schwab's notion of "commonplaces" in his 1971 *School Review* article, "The Practical: Translation into Curriculum." Chapter 2 has two sources: M. Cohen's Ohio State University master's thesis, "A Factor Analytic Study of Elementary School Student Teacher Concerns," as reported in Andrew Schwebel et al., *The Student Teacher Handbook* (Barnes & Noble, 1979), and Janet Sitter's dissertation from Michigan State University, titled "The Student Teaching Experience from the Perspective of the Student Teacher." Chapter 3 is based on Carl Grant and Ken Zeichner's "On Becoming a Reflective Teacher" from the book edited by Carl Grant titled *Preparing for Reflective Teaching: A Book of Readings* (Allyn & Bacon, 1984).

The exercises in Chapter 4 were inspired by books such as *Teaching Is . . .* by Merrill Harmin and Tom Gregory (SRA, 1974). Chapter 5 is based on many sources, including Tom Good and Jere Brophy's *Educational Psychology: A Realistic Approach*, 2nd ed. (Holt, Rinehart, and Winston, 1977), and Michael Young's *Knowledge and Control* (Collier-Macmillan, 1971). However, the basic structure of the chapter and the issues addressed are based on Ann Berlak and Harold Berlak's *Dilemmas of Schooling* (Methuen, 1981).

Chapter 6 uses ideas from Doug Roberts's "Developing the Concept of 'Curriculum Emphasis'" in *Science Education* (1982), and ideas of Ed Smith and Neil Sendelbach presented in "The Programme, the Plans and the Activities of the Classroom: The Demands of Activity-Based Science," a chapter in *Innovation in the Science Curriculum*, edited by John Olson (Nichols, 1982).

Chapter 7 draws on research carried out by Ken Zeichner and Bob Tabachnick at the University of Wisconsin–Madison (based on Berlak's work). Chapters 8 through 11 derive from Dan Lortie's *Schoolteacher* (University of Chicago Press, 1975), Willard Waller's *The Sociology of Teaching* (John Wiley and Sons, 1932), and Rob A. Walker and Clem Adelman's *A Guide to Classroom Observation* (Methuen, 1975).

Chapter 8 draws heavily on Ernest Stringer's model of action research and summarizes the model presented in *Action Research*, 3rd[d] ed. (Sage Publications, 2007).

Chapter 12 was developed by Laurie Vasily, currently a graduate student and co-instructor of a field-based course at Cornell University.

Beyond these specific contributions, the general orientation of the book derives from Ann Berlak and Harold Berlak's *Dilemmas of Schooling*, the many articles and papers on the student teaching experience, and reflective teaching by Ken Zeichner and company (including Bob Tabachnick and Carl Grant), then at the University of Wisconsin–Madison.

In addition to these major sources, criticisms by the following of earlier drafts have provided valuable help: Ken Zeichner and some of his students at the University of Wisconsin–Madison; Bill Schubert and his students at the University of Illinois, Chicago; Richard Duschel at the University of Pittsburgh; Ken Strike, Deborah Trumbull, and Joan Egner at Cornell; Jeff Dean and his colleagues and students at State University College at Oneonta; the faculty and students at Mansfield University;

and Al Rudnitsky and his students at Smith College. The observations of the reviewers of this edition—Cynthia L. Gissey, West Virginia University at Parkersburg; Jean Shepherd Hamm, East Tennessee State University; and Theresa Stewart, University of Illinois at Springfield—are also greatly appreciated.

The sixth edition benefited greatly from the comments and suggestions of Aram deKoven, who helped revise the text to make it more sensitive to the issues of technology, diversity, and learning differences.

This new seventh edition adds a new co-author, Craig Vivian, Associate Professor of Educational Studies at Monmouth College. Professor Vivian brings a background in action research, a strong grounding in foundational studies, as well as practical experience in teacher education. George Posner and Craig Vivian developed a close working relationship while the latter was a doctoral student at Cornell University, assisting in The Art of Teaching, the course that has served as the testing ground for this book for more than 25 years.

GEORGE J. POSNER

BRIEF CONTENTS

CONTENTS

PART ONE

Orientation

CHAPTER 1

Types of Field Experience*

The one indispensable part of any teacher preparation program is field experience. Student teaching can be considered a special type of field experience. It is so special that it is given a specific name and preferred status in preservice programs. In certain respects, however, all field experiences are similar. In this chapter, we will discuss some common features of all preservice field experiences. These common features will serve in subsequent chapters as a map on which to locate the concerns, goals, and issues faced by all students about to begin such experiences.

Common Features

All teaching situations have four features in common.[1] Although these four features may seem too obvious to mention or simply appear to reflect common sense, they will be useful reference points. First, almost by definition, a teaching situation must include a *teacher* or teachers of some sort. (The term *teaching agent* could be used to include texts or machines that teach, such as programmed instruction.) Second, there is at least one *learner* (termed *pupil* or *student*, depending on how old or how serious about learning the person is). Third, there is some *subject matter* or material that the teacher shares with, presents to, or negotiates with the learner; that is, there is something that the teacher teaches (the "stuff" of teaching), be it academic knowledge, personal feelings, or technical skills.

There is always a danger that a teaching situation will lack the necessary balance of these three features. When teaching ignores the learner, there is a tendency to be autocratic; when it ignores the teacher, it tends to be laissez-faire; when it ignores the subject matter, it is typically empty.

This "triad"[2] occurs within the fourth feature of a teaching situation—a social and physical *context*, consisting of rules, facilities, values, expectations, and personal backgrounds that act as resources, constraints, and direct influences on teaching and learning. Figure 1.1 summarizes these features.

When we think of teachers, learners, subject matter, and context, many issues come to mind. Each of these features serves as a category of issues for a discussion about educational topics. In fact, if these four features are truly comprehensive, we would expect all educational issues to fall into one or more of these categories.

---

*Written with Aram deKoven

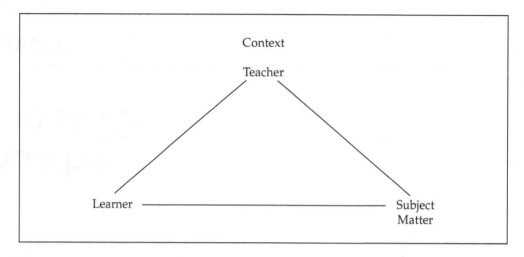

FIGURE 1.1   The four common features of teaching

Teachers

When we consider the teacher, we are addressing issues such as the following:

- The kind of person the teacher should be
- The proper role of the teacher
- The reasons people choose teaching as a career and stay in or leave the profession
- The reasons teachers burn out or remain fresh
- The tasks teachers face in classrooms

Learners

In a sense, we are and will always be learners, regardless of our age or position. Obviously, the range of potential learners is immense, particularly if we consider not only ages but also purposes, aspirations, and backgrounds. We must also consider that this diversity greatly affects any teaching. Furthermore, there is quite a difference between teaching in a one-on-one situation and teaching a large group of diverse individuals. In one-on-one (or one-to-*small* group) situations, issues such as the following arise regarding the learner:

- What the learner already knows
- What comes easily or with difficulty
- What learners consider to be relevant
- The anxieties that must be taken into account
- The learner's future career
- What the learner is likely to find interesting, stimulating, or challenging
- The cultural background of the learner

When teaching a group of learners, additional issues arise:

- The treatment of learners as unique individuals or as members of categories (e.g., gifted and talented, non-college bound)
- The degree to which learners should be treated equally or differently
- Whether the fastest, the middle, or the slowest learners should be used as a reference for decisions about when to move on to new material (i.e., pacing)

- How the teacher should try to develop a sense of "groupness," while respecting learner individuality
- How to help both learners eager to participate and those reluctant to participate

Subject Matter

What teachers teach ranges from facts and concepts to thinking processes, to physical skills, to values and to feelings. One issue of concern is the relative importance of each of these domains of subject matter. For example, we might question the legitimacy of using the teacher's or the learner's own feelings as subject matter for instruction. Or we might try to decide whether to regard subject matter as truths to be learned or to emphasize how truth is reached.

Another important issue concerns the fact that time is a scarce commodity. We simply do not have time to teach everything as completely as desired. Therefore, we always seem to be faced with the "breadth versus depth" issue. For example, how much should we try to cover, and to what extent should we take the time to get all the students to understand the material fully? How do we reconcile these often conflicting demands for coverage and mastery? What impact does the material we omit have for students of differing abilities, interests, and backgrounds?

Context

Classrooms are unique places that do not change very much. They have distinctive physical and social qualities that persist from generation to generation. In terms of physical qualities, they have significant similarities and differences. Philip Jackson[3] asks us to imagine entering a school at night, with nobody else there and all the lights off. The smell alone would tell us where we are. The distinctive smells of cleaning fluids, chalk dust, and pencil shavings would give it away. Turning on the lights would confirm our location:

> School bulletin boards may be changed but they are never discarded, the seats may be arranged but 30 of them are there to stay, the teacher's desk may have a new plant on it but there it sits, as ubiquitous as the roll-down maps, the olive drab wastebaskets, and the pencil sharpener on the window ledge.[4]

However, there is also great diversity among schools. Jonathon Kozol graphically describes the shocking differences in facilities between rich and poor schools (especially those in adjacent districts) and the impact of these differences on the education of children.

In terms of social context, the classroom is also highly unique and stable. The makeup of classes and the faculty does not change drastically during the year. The conditions are almost always crowded. "Only in schools do thirty or more people spend several hours each day literally side by side. Once we leave the classroom we seldom are required to have contact with so many people for so long a time."[5] The daily schedule, types of classroom activity (e.g., seatwork, teacher demonstration), and rules (e.g., "keep your eyes on your own paper during tests") are highly uniform:

> Life [in school] resembles life in other contexts in some ways, but not all. There is, in other words, a uniqueness to the student's world. School, like church and home, is someplace special. Look where you may, you will not find another place quite like it.[6]

Context includes all that constrains, facilitates, or otherwise influences what teachers and learners do with subject matter. Context, therefore, includes the immediate physical and social environment of the classroom. But it also includes the administration of the school, parental influences, the media (especially television), laws, court decisions, governmental regulations, the backgrounds of learners and teachers, the money available to finance education, and the time available for teaching.

From a broader viewpoint, the school is one of society's most pervasive institutions and, as such, can be held responsible for any contribution it may have made to societal problems. Even if the school is not responsible for these problems, some people see it as a powerful force for reforming society.

Teaching and learning take place in institutions and agencies other than schools, which typically have contexts quite dissimilar from classrooms. For example, the 4-H program, the Boy Scouts, the Girl Scouts, and other youth groups may each take place in different venues. That is, they may have different physical contexts. However, the social context of these programs may have some similar elements including rituals, pledges, and/or oaths. However, the social context of a program in different locations may have similarities based on common rituals, pledges, oaths, and other procedures. Nevertheless, to some extent each program site has a unique social context determined by its unique set of participants and staff.

Issues derived from the contextual aspects of teaching include the following:

- The amount of input that parents should have in the program of the school or group
- The extent to which the problems facing teachers and learners are due to problems in the society at large, in the organization of schools, in the individual learner, or in the learner's family
- The extent to which the teacher or group leader can or should criticize the policies and practices of the government, the schools, the youth group or agency, or other teachers or co-workers, and the extent to which the teacher or group leaders should try to encourage such criticism by the learner
- The value of using the community at large as an educational resource

The Four Common Features as a Whole

It would be difficult, if not impossible, to think of teaching without any one of these four features. Teaching without someone or something doing the teaching sounds absurd. Teaching without someone to teach sounds like a charade. Teaching without something to teach sounds like a waste of everybody's time. Teaching without any context is impossible.

Not only are all the features necessary, they are also of equal importance. These four features comprise the whole of the phenomenon we call education.[7] Any particular conception of education—whether psychological, sociological, or philosophical—provides at best one perspective of this whole and, more typically, one perspective on one facet of the whole. Care must be exercised if we are to maintain an approach that includes the whole of teaching. Concern with maintaining our role as teachers should not blind us to the ways in which the learner learns best. Concern for covering the subject matter should not blind us to the needs of the learners. Concern for the learner's feelings should not obscure the community's expectations and the value of learning the subject matter. Neither the learner, nor the subject matter, nor the physical and social content, nor our own needs as teachers should be allowed to dominate. All features must be coordinated to achieve a balance.

The set of four features provides a map on which to locate each concern relative to the others. The set not only suggests that from each perspective we will "see *some* part of the whole . . . [but also] enables [us] to know—to some degree, at any rate—*what* part of the whole [we] will see."[8]

The common features of teaching have been expressed in somewhat abstract terms in order to make them an all-purpose way of discussing any teaching situation. Now we will try to make them more concrete.

Varieties of Teaching Situations

No two field experiences are identical. One way to describe their differences is to refer to the four common features. We shall begin by examining the range of experiences you have already had (using the four common features) and conclude by identifying the types of experiences you are lacking.

When students in one of my classes were about to embark on an exploratory field experience, I asked for an inventory of their previous teaching experience. They responded with a wide range of teaching situations:

- Teaching first aid to kindergarten classes
- Teaching balloon sculpturing to college classmates
- Teaching long-duration hiking to a 4-H group
- Teaching piano to a sister
- Being a counselor at the county jail
- Tutoring a tenth-grader in history
- Teaching a little brother to bowl
- Teaching horseback riding to kids ages 4 to 15 at summer camp
- Teaching a younger brother how to tie his shoes
- Coaching the debate team
- Teaching new routines and correcting moves as a sergeant in the color guard
- Teaching a friend how to change a car's oil
- Teaching a sister the evils of cigarette smoking (or trying to)
- Teaching a driver-education class on drunken driving
- Teaching backgammon to Mother
- Teaching Morse code in the Navy
- Teaching a friend to meditate

EXERCISE 1.1

Inventory of Teaching Experiences

You probably have had more experience as a teacher than you realize. Maybe you took charge of a group such as scouts, 4-H, summer camp, or a club in high school. If you were responsible for what the group learned from the experience, you were a teacher. Maybe you tried to tutor someone. You might have been an official tutor. Or perhaps your friend, brother, or sister needed something explained or demonstrated. Even as a babysitter, you might have had to explain or demonstrate something occasionally. The subject matter might have ranged from algebra to sharing toys to tying shoes. This exercise is intended to help inventory past experience as a teacher. Completing it should result in a greater awareness of previous teaching experience and a more informal basis for choosing future field experiences. Use Form 1.1 to list your teaching experiences.

The experiences spanned a wide range of learners, subject matter, and contexts. The learners ranged from 4-year-old children to a 40-year-old mother. The subject matter ranged from physical skills (such as shoe tying, bowling, piano playing, and changing a car's oil), to factual knowledge (such as history and Morse code), to attitudes and values (such as emotional problems of prisoners and the evils of cigarette smoking), to intellectual skills (such as debating). The contexts ranged from 1:1 tutoring and counseling to 1:30 teaching and from educational institutions such as schools and colleges, to youth groups and service agencies (4-H, Big Brothers, etc.), to families and friendships, and even to the armed forces.

(continued)

EXERCISE **1.1** **Continued**

FORM 1.1   **Inventory of teaching experiences**

Experience	Subject matter	Learner's age or grade level	Context (e.g., school, camp, youth group)	Ways different from you (e.g., racial, cultural, socioeconomic)
0.	Swimming	Ages 7–9	Summer camp	City kids
1.				
2.				
3.				
4.				
5.				

It might be useful to examine each of your prior teaching experiences in terms of the learners, the subject matter, and the context in order to determine their range. Also consider your range of teaching experiences with people different from yourself. Use the space provided in Form 1.1 to identify these features of your experiences. How wide is your range of experiences? What types of experiences do you lack? Are any of these worth pursuing at this time?
▶*

Variety of Field Experiences

In some field-oriented courses, students have a wide choice of placements available to them. In other courses, field placements are chosen for the student. Whatever the situation, it is doubtful that you will have as much choice as you would like. Options are never limitless. Furthermore, rarely in life do we find ourselves in the "perfect" situation. For all these reasons, regardless of your degree of placement choice, the most productive attitude is to "bloom where you are planted," that is, to be a motivated professional in any circumstance.

One way to make certain that the environment in which you find yourself permits you to "bloom" is to look for ways in which you can adjust to the situation and in which you can adapt the placement to address your goals and concerns (see Chapter 2). Most teaching situations will allow you some flexibility.

We examine variety in field experiences as a means of thinking about this idea of mutual adaptation as well as field-placement choice.

Teacher.   Field experiences vary greatly in the roles expected of both the teacher and of you, a student functioning as the teacher's co-worker. At one extreme, the field placement might offer you the rather limited but frequently profitable role of observer, without your engaging in any real teaching. At the other extreme, you might find yourself in the more intensive role of teacher-in-charge, without much contact with other adults. Between these two extremes is the role of teacher's aide or assistant teacher.

---

*The reader will notice arrows like this one used throughout the text. They indicate that a reader response is expected.

How much autonomy you want and how active a role you want to play are two key issues you need to address in your planning. Perhaps, you will be able to work out an arrangement by which you begin as an observer and gradually increase your teaching responsibilities as the semester progresses. This might be a good time to jot down your preferences for your field experience.

What kind of relationship with an experienced teacher do you prefer in your field placement? Do you want to teach actively? What sorts of tasks do you want to make sure that you tackle in your field experience? For example, do you want to plan lessons; deal with discipline problems; lead a discussion; give a lecture; supervise group activities; help individuals having problems; observe a variety of methods; or design, administer, or correct a test? How much help do you think you will need with each of these tasks?

▶

Learners. In general, a good guiding principle is to try to work with learners whose backgrounds are different from your own. The more you learn about other people and ways to teach them, the more versatile a teacher you will become. One key issue to address is the age of the learners with whom you would like to work. Depending on the opportunities available, the learners could conceivably range from 3-year-olds (e.g., in a daycare facility) to elderly people (e.g., in a nursing home). Besides age, there are other characteristics to consider when selecting a field placement or making the most of the field site in which you are placed. You might have a particular interest in working with learners who have special problems or needs (e.g., children with learning disabilities), learners with particular backgrounds (e.g., refugees), or learners with special interests and aptitudes (e.g., gifted and talented).

With what sorts of learners might you work? How old? What type of family backgrounds? Any special physical, emotional, or intellectual characteristics? (For more information about learners see Chapter 10.)

▶

Subject Matter. Whether you realize it or not, you know a great deal. In fact, you probably even have substantial expertise in some areas. Take the time now to think about some of your areas of expertise. Consider not only your knowledge in academic subjects (e.g., your major), but also skills, such as athletics, computing, writing, arts and crafts, photography, drawing, music, and theater. This is a time to draw on your extracurricular activities. Don't forget that besides the obvious skills, there are others we often take for granted, such as reading and speaking, using the library, and everyday survival skills (e.g., opening and maintaining a checking account). Many undergraduates assume that they do not have expertise in anything until they begin to think more deeply about what they know and can do. The important point is to try to make sure that your field experience puts you in the position of teaching what you know well. You teach in your field experience, even if you first need to do some research in order to build up weak areas.

What subject matter might you teach? Physical skills, attitudes, values, feelings? Facts and concepts? Intellectual skills? A mixture of these or some other type of subject matter? Might you teach academic subject matter or life skills needed to get along after schooling?

▶

Context.   The setting in which you teach may affect the quality of your field experience. For example, teaching in a school is quite different from teaching in a youth group (such as Girl Scouts). If you have a choice in the selection of your field placement, you will need to decide whether you want to broaden your experiences or seek a field placement in an organization with which you have previous experience. Or, if teaching in a school is your eventual goal, you might want to get your feet wet in a classroom. Regardless of the organization, whether school or community agency, now is also the time to consider whether you would rather work one-on-one with a single learner (e.g., tutoring) or with groups of learners. Clearly, the larger the group, the less opportunity you will have to spend time with each individual. Also, management of the learners becomes a more significant issue with larger groups, although this also depends on the ability and willingness of the learners to work together cooperatively.

In what context might the teaching take place? Individual or group? In what institution? Schools? Curricular or extracurricular? What levels? Social agencies? Youth groups? Any special characteristics of the context, for example, size of group?
▶

The Student Teaching Experience

Seen within this framework of teachers, learners, subject matter, and context, student teaching is a very special type of field experience.

Learners

The learners may come from a wide range of socioeconomic and ethnic backgrounds, some of which may be quite foreign to student teachers. The learners may also represent a broad spectrum of abilities and may range from those bordering on the developmentally delayed to those considered to be geniuses. To some extent, every student teaching experience is unique because every learner is unique.

Subject Matter

With the extent of their backgrounds in some school subject matter, some student teachers take that subject matter for granted, believing that others consider it significant, straightforward, interesting, and not too difficult to learn. It is important to remember, however, that most of the subject matter taught in schools is taught nowhere else and, therefore, is somewhat esoteric. In addition, English, social studies, science, math, art, or physical education may be easy and fun for a person who has majored in the subject but may be difficult or boring for many others. Furthermore, the learners' parents may have learned something very different in the subject when they attended school. Finally, student teachers may conceive of the subject matter in terms of just facts and concepts, but they are also teaching values and attitudes, if not explicitly, then at least by example and by use of stated and unstated classroom rules. (See Chapter 5 for a more extended discussion of the "hidden curriculum.")

Context

Of the four features, the social context and, in particular, the role of the student teacher most distinguish student teaching from all other teaching situations. A student teacher can be considered a junior partner to the cooperating teacher.[9] This role restricts both a student teacher's classroom responsibilities and opportunities for experimentation. A student teacher is not typically seen as an equal member of a teaching team, a role some professional teachers achieve; nor is a student teacher autonomous, a role most professional teachers prefer; nor is a student teacher merely an aide because cooperating teachers typically expect student teachers to assume increased responsibility during the term. To complicate matters further, a student teacher answers not only to the cooperating teacher but also to the college supervisor. A student teacher is still a college student and, typically, the college supervisor assigns a grade based on the supervisor's observations and the cooperating teacher's recommendations. It is unlikely that a student teacher will ever again be in a situation quite like this one. It is at the same time exciting, frustrating, and ultimately fulfilling.[10]

Placement Tips

As you embark on your field placement assignments, you should be excited. Many students describe their field placements as being among the most memorable experiences of their college careers. At the same time, many students also recall their placements as very challenging.

Remember, young people need many factors to be in place to develop optimally. One factor that appears to be more important than the others is the presence of at least one positive adult role model.[11] As a volunteer placed in an educational setting, you may have the opportunity to serve as a mentor to a youth. I am sure that you will find this task tremendously rewarding but also not without its challenges. Here are five tips that you may find helpful to consider prior to beginning your assignment working with youths and young adults. These tips can be especially useful when working with an at-risk population, a population that is likely already predisposed to resist your attempts to form close and constructive relationships.

- Don't try to be best friends overnight. Building a relationship with anybody takes time; this fact is especially true with many at-risk youths. Set your expectations appropriately and be patient. Stay alert and tuned into the comfort levels of the student or students with whom you are working. Be prepared and willing to take detours from the core subject matter that you have prepared. Sometimes, in order to talk meaningfully about a student's troubles in school, you first have to talk about what he or she is good at and enjoys, whether that be fishing, sports, motocross racing, or soap operas.
- Be reliable. Trust takes time to develop and is essential to a working, healthy, and productive relationship with a child. At-risk teens can be less willing to trust others than are young people who are not considered at risk.[12] With this in mind, it is important to seize every opportunity to build trust. For starters, this means being on time, calling if plans change, and not making promises that cannot be kept.
- Try to withhold judgment. Young people's minds operate differently from adults' minds, and this can frequently be the basis for countless disagreements and misunderstandings between adults and youths. The adolescent brain is prone to react to stimuli in ways that, to you, will seem to circumvent reason, intellect, and common sense.[13] In order to stimulate conversation and openness, it is helpful to do more listening than critiquing, at least early on in your relationship. There will no doubt be times when it is hard to stifle your thoughts and observations; however, I suggest that you wait until asked for your thoughts before attempting to share them. If you have good ideas for young people, by all means share them, but wait until the door to them is open.
- Be yourself. If you try to be something you are not, you run the risk of jeopardizing the trust you will need to be forming. Frequently, mentors express a concern

that their protégés will not like them. It has been my experience that the only way to facilitate a young person to like you is to start by being honest about who you are to them. Don't try to be cool, hip, or "down with that"; just be the caring person you are.

■ Be optimistic, supportive, and caring. Not much needs to be said about this category because surely this one is common sense. The more you enjoy what you are doing, the more other people will enjoy themselves being around you, and the more you will enjoy yourself. Try it—you'll find it to be an exquisite cycle!

In addition to these five tips mentioned, here are a few more points you should consider as you begin thinking about your field placement. I recommend that you be open with youths about the duration of your stay with them. Many of you will be placed with youths for a semester. This *is* enough time for meaningful bonds to form. If you are not open in the beginning of your placement about your overall time commitment, youths may in the end feel betrayed, or at least there may be hurt feelings. This may be especially true for at-risk youths, who may already have serious issues with abandonment and feelings of betrayal. Taking this step at the beginning of your relationship demonstrates a genuine interest in openness on your part. This step in turn can enhance the depth of your relationship and can make things easier for you and your students when the semester comes to an end. In addition, it can make life for future volunteers and professionals who show up in this young person's life seeking to act as role models easier and more productive in a shorter amount of time.

While in your placement, you will need to be thinking not only about the relationships you will be building with youths but also about the relationship you are building with the institution with which you are working. As a volunteer in a placement setting, you are an ambassador representing the school or organization from which you come. What this means is that you should work to maintain good rapport with your site supervisors and with other key people. You should be professional, courteous, and reliable. If, for some reason, you need to leave your placement earlier than expected, make your plans known in a timely fashion to both your site supervisor and the youths with whom you are working. Don't just fail to show up. In order to leave the best possible impression, I suggest writing a thank-you note or leaving a small gift for your site supervisor at the end of your placement. Remember, the legacy you leave at your field placement site will either help or hinder future students who wish to have the same wonderful experience that you had working with young people.

Important: During your interactions with young people, you may be presented with information about abuse or neglect. If this should happen to you, you may be required either legally or ethically to report certain types of information directly to school or organization officials. Situations in which a young person describes to you plans to hurt himself or herself or others, or when someone is hurting the student, either in the past, present, or future, it is required that you act and share this information with the appropriate officials. Check with your teacher and/or your site supervisor about legal requirements and what the appropriate course of actions should be. Do not attempt to act as a psychologist or counselor yourself. You will do no harm to the student if you are a good listener, open, and caring in the moment and then refer the situation to a person who has proper training to deal with it.

Sadly, many youths do not have even one reliable, loving, and supportive adult figure with whom to share the trials and tribulations of adolescence.[14] In addition, consider that many communities and parents seem to have lost much of their power and/or willingness to be involved with the rearing of children, and that TV, movies, and the Internet have moved in to fill the gap by becoming new and powerful sources for knowledge, values, and behaviors for youths.[15] In your field placement, you can (even though for a short period of time) provide a young person at least with something to look forward to and at best with a life-altering experience. I hope that you will use the opportunity to impart the wisdom of tolerance, acceptance, and the quest for knowledge and understanding to young people. Never before have we as a society been in such need of people to act as positive role models for youths. You can help.

One last point to remember that may be helpful: Many people doing labors of love never get the thanks they deserve. In your fieldwork placements, you may never be thanked by the young people with whom you work; however, remember that if you give this experience your best shot, your name may be the name spoken in a decade's time, as the person who gave the impetus to make positive life-altering changes.

NOTES

1. See Joseph Schwab, "The Practical: Arts of Eclectic," *School Review* 79 (August 1971), 493–542. He terms my four common features "commonplaces."
2. David Hawkins, "I, Thou, It," *Mathematics Teaching, Journal of the British Association of Teachers of Mathematics*, 46 (Spring 1969).
3. Philip Jackson, *Life in Classrooms* (New York: Holt, Rinehart and Winston, 1968).
4. Ibid., pp. 6–7.
5. Ibid., p. 8.
6. Ibid., p. 9.
7. See Schwab, "The Practical," for the source of this discussion.
8. Ibid., p. 339 (italics in original).
9. Janet Sitter and Perry Lanier, "Student Teaching: A Stage in the Development of a Teacher? Or a Period of Consolidation?" Paper presented at the annual meeting of the American Educational Research Association, New York, March 1982.
10. D. John McIntyre, David Byrd, and Susan Foxx, "Field and Laboratory Experiences," in *Handbook of Research on Teacher Education*, 2nd ed., ed. John Sikula (New York: Macmillan, 1996), pp. 173–174.
11. Emmy E. Werner and R. S. Smith, *Kauai's Children Come of Age* (Honolulu, HI: University of Hawaii Press, 1977); J. Garbarino, *Raising Children in a Socially Toxic Environment* (San Francisco: Jossey-Bass, 1995).
12. J. Rhoded, W. L. Haight, et al., "The Influence of Mentoring on the Peer Relationships of Foster Youth in Relative and Non-Relative Care," *Journal of Research on Adolescents*, 9(2) (1999), 185–201.
13. Carter, R., *Mapping the Mind* (London: Weildenfeld and Nicholson, 1998); M. Nerney, *What Can We Do to Protect Our Youth from Drugs and Alcohol?* (Ithaca, NY: publisher, 1998); Stepp, L., *Our Last Best Shot: Guiding Our Children Through Early Adolescence* (New York: Riverhead Books, 2000); J. Garbarino, *Raising Children in a Socially Toxic Environment* (San Francisco: Jossey-Bass, 1995).
14. P.C. Scales, "A Responsive Ecology for Positive Young Adolescent Development," *The Clearing House*, 69(4) (1996), 226.
15. D. Ravitch and J. P. Viteritti, eds., *Kids Stuff: Marketing Sex and Violence to America's Children* (Baltimore: The John Hopkins University Press, 2003).

CHAPTER 2

Concerns and Personal Goals

If you are feeling a bit anxious about your field experiences, you are not alone. It may come as a surprise to learn that most of the other students about to embark on a field experience are similarly concerned. However, with some deliberate thought on the matter, you may be able to translate your anxieties and concerns into personal goals. This chapter is intended to help make explicit the concerns you have as you anticipate your field experience and discover the feelings of other people in similar situations. Finally, this chapter will help you to identify personal goals you might want to achieve during your field experience.

EXERCISE 2.1

Expressing Concerns

Take a moment to express your primary concerns regarding your field experience. What worries you or occupies your mind about it? For example, in what ways do you feel that you will not measure up? That the experience will not be what you really want? In what ways do you feel that you will be disappointed? What really counts for your satisfaction with the experience? Make a list of these concerns in the space provided.
▶

1.
2.
3.
4.
5.
6.

Analyzing Concerns

Now we will analyze expressed concerns by using the four features of teaching (from Chapter 1) as categories of analysis. This will help stimulate further thinking about concerns.

Teachers

Concern with being a competent professional typically involves being knowledgeable; being perceived as competent, reflective, and decisive; and continually improving one's methods. Consider the following concerns, taken from a study of elementary teachers.[1] The numbers in parentheses give the percentages of the 139 elementary school student teachers surveyed who reported these concerns as causing them moderate to very great concern:

- Not falling into routine methods of presenting material (69.1)
- Finding ways of keeping up with new ideas in education (57.5)
- Achieving a good understanding of personal strengths and weaknesses with respect to teaching (56.8)

Learners

Who the learners are, what they are like, and how to respond to them as individuals are likely to be the areas of concern. For example, the same study of elementary teachers found the following:

- Discovering and developing the potential talents of each child (76.3)
- Presenting the work in ways that engage the students' interest (74.0)
- Adapting assignments to the needs of the individual student (69.8)
- Working with students who don't seem to care if they learn (81.3)

Subject Matter

Teaching subject matter effectively is usually an area of concern expressed in terms of covering the material and helping learners to understand and apply it. For example, the same study of elementary teachers found the following:

- Teaching students to think through problems on their own (71.2)
- Finding sufficient time to cover the required material effectively (61.2)
- Getting students to apply what they have learned to new problems (63.3)
- Presenting material in ways that foster understanding (64.0)

Context

Concern for effectively managing groups of learners involves establishing and enforcing rules, creating a climate conducive to learning, maintaining it, and restoring it constructively when necessary.[2] Such a climate is necessary to minimize the disruptive effects that one individual can have on the group and to maximize the educational benefits to all members of the group. For example, the study of elementary teachers found the following:

- Finding ways to control the students effectively (72.6)
- Dealing with students who interfere with others' work (70.4)
- Providing all the pupils with opportunities for class participation (55.4)
- Dealing with classroom troublemakers (68.4)

Although these concerns are expressed in classroom terms, they apply to work within any group context (e.g., Boy Scouts). In one-to-one teaching situations, such as tutoring, concerns might include the following:

- Maintaining support from the teacher and the family
- Finding a place to work with minimal distractions
- Finding the necessary resources

Do your expressed concerns refer primarily to the learners, the subject matter, the context, or yourself as a professional teacher? How similar are your concerns to those of others beginning a preservice field experience?

▶

Expressing Goals

(Your) Concerns about your upcoming field experience will greatly affect the ways in which you will benefit from it. Serious concerns can become anxieties and uncertainties that can lead to nervousness or even depression. Nobody wants that. Instead, the analysis of concerns is intended to increase the benefit of the field experience. In order for you to benefit from an examination of concerns, however, you must translate the concerns into actions. In order to do this, you have to formulate goals and plans, based on your concerns.

For example, if you are concerned that you will not be able to present material in ways that engage students' interest, you might want to formulate the goal of developing the skills needed to present material in interesting ways. Or, if you are concerned that you will not be able to control students effectively, your goal might be to see if you can control students effectively. Making these goals explicit can be a productive exercise.

EXERCISE 2.2

Expressing Personal Goals and Priorities

Our goals affect our actions, expectations, and perceptions. This happens even when we are not explicitly aware of our goals. By expressing our goals, we can examine them and decide whether they are useful for us at that time.

Write a few sentences, describing how you expect to benefit from your field experience, based on the concerns you expressed in the previous section.

▶

Now look at what you have written. You might want to compare your goals with the following goals mentioned by my students:

1. To find out what teaching is really like (i.e., career exploration)
2. To see if I like teaching (i.e., exploring personal preferences)
3. To see if I can really do it (i.e., self-testing)
4. To learn some skills and modify certain habits and characteristics (i.e., training)
5. To develop my own approach or style (i.e., personal style)
6. To apply what I've learned in college to real students and to real classrooms (i.e., theory into practice)

Try considering each of your goals as a variation or specific case of one of the aforementioned six general goal types. If this matching does no violence to your goals, label your goals 1–6, according to which general goal type each represents. Try to rank order your own goals or the six goal types listed here according to how important each is to you for this particular field experience.

▶

EXERCISE **2.2 Continued**

1.

2.

3.

4.

5.

6.

What do you conclude? Do you view your field experience primarily as exploratory (goals 1 and 2), as a time to test yourself (goal 3), as a training period (goal 4), as a search for personal identity (goal 5), or as an extension of your college education (goal 6)? Where are your current priorities?

▶

Goals may be experienced sequentially. Early field experiences might be exploratory (goals 1 and 2) and offer an opportunity to get your feet wet, to examine teaching from the other side of the desk. The next set of field experiences might provide a chance to learn some techniques of teaching (goal 4 and perhaps goal 5). These intermediate field experiences can serve as a time to learn everything possible about teaching. Courses late in the teacher education program might provide a knowledge base on which to teach (goal 6). Janet Sitter[3] found just such a progression in the "interns" she supervised. She found, however, that as they began to prepare for student teaching, their goals changed. "She no longer expressed a desire to learn all there is to know. . . . Now [that] she had been taught to teach, it was her task to go into the classroom and prove that she had learned; that she could do it."[4] That is, the students began to view student teaching less as "practice teaching" (goal 4), and more as a "proving ground" (goal 3). I mention this progression from goal 4 to goal 3 not as something student teachers should strive for but only as an example of the way people shift goals during their teacher preparation program. Goals are tentative, not permanent.

For some students, developing a personal style or approach (goal 5) might be relevant at every level of their program. For others, it might not be seriously considered until their second or third year of regular employment, after they have survived the often traumatic first year of professional teaching. However, regardless of the pressure and intensity of the experience, goal 5 is certainly compatible with all the others and is a worthwhile ongoing goal for every field experience.

EXERCISE **2.3**

Setting Specific Goals

Once you have formulated personal goals to guide your field experience, it might be productive to set more specific goals. In order to do this, consider again each of the general goal types and the specific concerns you expressed earlier.

Goal 1: To find out what teaching is really like
Are there some specific kinds of teaching situations you would like to explore? (Refer to your responses on page 8 in Chapter 1.)

(continued)

EXERCISE **2.3** **Continued**

Teacher.   Would you like to work with or under a particular type of teacher? One with a certain philosophy or approach? One with a special type of training or background? A particular ethnic background?
▶

Learners.   Are there some specific kinds of learners about whom you want to learn? Learners with special problems? Gifted or talented learners? Particular ages? Particular ethnic backgrounds?
▶

Subject matter.   Is there some particular subject matter you want to try teaching? A particular school subject? A sport? Do you have some specialty you want to try?
▶

Context.   Are there any contexts that you want to explore? Particular youth groups or social agencies? Particular size groups? Team teaching? Open classrooms? Communities with special characteristics?
▶

Goal 2: To see if you really like teaching
Are there some specific types of teaching activities you want to try? These might include leading a discussion, giving a lecture, setting up a role-play, one-to-one tutoring, helping a child with personal problems, discussing a controversial issue with a class, dealing with a disruptive child, assigning grades, meeting with a parent, designing and teaching a unit or a lesson, setting up and then teaching a laboratory lesson, or doing a demonstration.
▶

Goal 3: To see if you can really do it
To whom do you want to prove yourself? To yourself? To a group of learners? To your college supervisor? To parents? To the cooperating teacher? To aides? Do you want to "lead" and be recognized as "the leader"? Be recognized by whom?
▶

For many teachers in training, when others recognize their leadership, they report "feeling like a teacher."[5] Developing a teacher identity plays an important role in proving oneself.[6]

Goal 4: To learn some skills and modify certain habits and characteristics
What particular skills do you want to learn? What instructional techniques?
▶

EXERCISE 2.3 Continued

Your goals may derive from what you regard as the keys to successful teaching. For example, most student teachers attribute successful teaching either to general good planning or to well-executed lessons, although some also specify "challenging" or "interesting" lessons, those they enjoy themselves, giving clear directions, and providing variety (change of pace).[7] Developing these sorts of teaching skills might be important to you. In addition to instructional techniques, organization and management techniques might have a high priority. For Sitter's[8] student teachers, this meant:

> successfully getting a group of learners through a lesson or series of lessons within a limited amount of time. It meant creating a classroom climate conducive to learning; maintaining the environment and restoring the climate constructively when necessary.[9]

In addition to skills, are there certain habits, traits, or characteristics that you want to acquire or modify? Do you believe, as did some of Sitter's[10] student teachers, that your ability to teach will be hindered by a "lack of patience, low tolerance level, shyness, inadequate feelings, insecurities,"[11] "poor time assessment, lack of creativity, general lack of knowledge in either the scope or sequence of content,"[12] "lack of ambition, hyperactivity, aggressiveness, or lack of commitment"?[13] Obviously, attempts to change such personal propensities are at best frustrating and at worst impossible. But identifying them and explicitly working on them in a field experience might at least allow you to accept them and then to compensate for them.
▶

Goal 5: To develop your own approach or style
What makes you unique as a teacher? What do you stand for and believe in?
▶

This goal is something you will achieve as you work through this book. Your own personal perspective on teaching is, in one sense, your own approach. What approaches to, or styles of, teaching would you like to learn about in the process of developing your own? Can you find anyone who epitomizes your ideal teacher?
▶

Goal 6: To apply what you have learned in college to real learners and to real classrooms
Are there any specific concepts or theories you want to apply—for example, theories of group dynamics, developmental theories, personality theories, learning theories, motivational theories, or sociological theories? What will you look for in your field experience in order to make the application?
▶

Having considered all these goals, try to specify your personal goals and list them in order of priority.
▶

For example, consider the following goals mentioned by one prospective elementary school student teacher:

- To learn more about implementing a language-experience approach to reading
- To work on some sort of "discipline technique"—learning to feel out where you have to draw the line and how far it can go before you have to start saying "all right, sit down," etc.

(continued)

EXERCISE **2.3** **Continued**

- To become more sensitive to the feelings and needs of individual children ("getting to know the children faster")
- To develop more confidence as a teacher—specifically, wanting to develop the ability to "change course" in the middle of a lesson when the children do not respond to what has been planned

Keeping your goals in mind, write down your plans to reach these goals, or at least to move in that direction.

NOTES

1. Andrew Schwebel, Bernice Schwebel, Carol Schwebel, and Milton Schwebel, *The Student Teacher Handbook* (New York: Barnes & Noble, 1979), pp. 20–24.
2. Janet Sitter, "The Student Teaching Experience from the Perspective of the Student Teacher: A Descriptive Study." Unpublished doctoral dissertation, Michigan State University, 1982.
3. Ibid.
4. Ibid., p. 127.
5. Ibid.
6. Ibid.
7. Ibid., pp. 136–139.
8. Ibid.
9. Ibid., p. 139.
10. Ibid.
11. Ibid., p. 148.
12. Ibid., p. 149.
13. Ibid.

CHAPTER 3

Reflecting on Field Experiences: Fieldwork Logs

Experience + Reflection = Growth

As this equation suggests (and as John Dewey has argued), we do not actually learn from experience as much as we learn from reflecting on experience. Reflection on an experience, to put it simply, means thinking about the experience, what the experience means, how it felt, where it might lead, and what to do about it.

This chapter will help you to document and begin to reflect on your field experience. There are many possible ways to become more reflective about teaching. This book uses two methods: in-text questions/exercises and logs or journals. Before these methods are explained, however, an explanation of reflective thinking is necessary.

What Is Reflective Thinking, and Why Is It Desirable?

According to the educational philosopher John Dewey, reflective thinking means "turning a subject over in the mind and giving it serious and consecutive consideration."[1] Dewey insists that reflective thinking frees us from mere "impulsive" and "routine activity."[2] It enables us to act in "deliberate and intentional fashion" to achieve what we need. It distinguishes us as human beings and is the hallmark of intelligent (as opposed to mere "appetitive, blind and impulsive") action.[3]

Nonreflective teachers rely on routine behavior and are guided more by impulse, tradition, and authority than by reflection. They simplify their professional lives by uncritically accepting everyday reality in schools. They can then "concentrate their efforts on finding the most effective and efficient means to achieve ends and to solve problems that have largely been defined for them by others."[4] In contrast, reflective teachers actively, persistently, and carefully consider and reconsider beliefs and practices "in light of the grounds that support them and the further consequences to which they lead."[5]

Reflective thinking allows a teacher to examine critically the assumptions that schools make about what can count as acceptable goals and methods, problems, and solutions. Although we all must live within some constraints, often we accept as predetermined by authority or tradition far more than is necessary.[6]

In your field experience, reflective thinking will allow you to act in deliberate and intentional ways, devise new ways of teaching rather than always falling back on tradition, and interpret new experiences from a fresh perspective. A reflective teacher is able to see problems from a student's point of view and tries to understand a situation as a problem that has been framed incorrectly by the learner. Because a reflective teacher treats every student's conditions of learning as being unique to that student, the usual teaching approaches do not work. Teacher and student must work together to reframe the learning situation.[7]

As suggested by the equation at the beginning of this chapter, reflection with no experience is sterile and generally leads to unworkable conclusions. Experience with no reflection is shallow and at best leads to superficial knowledge. If you merely "do" your field experience without thinking deeply about it, if you merely allow your experiences to wash over you without savoring and examining them for their significance, then your growth will be greatly limited. The logs you write, the questions you try to answer, and other activities in which you engage are all merely tools to facilitate reflective thinking about your field experience.

Is It Possible for an Effective Teacher to Reflect?

As necessary as reflective teaching may seem to some people, others are unconvinced. They argue that there is no *time* for reflection if at the same time you must teach effectively, that there is no *point* for reflection if you always have to do what you are told anyway, and that reflection is not *necessary* because you can be a good teacher without it. Let us examine these three objections one at a time.[8]

Is There Time?   Philip Jackson[9] reminds us that classrooms are busy places:

> [An elementary] teacher engages in as many as 1000 interpersonal interchanges each day. . . . Teaching commonly involves talking and the teacher acts as a gatekeeper who manages the flow of the classroom dialogue. . . . Another time-consuming task for the teacher . . . is that of serving as supply sergeant. Classroom space and material resources are limited and the teacher must allocate these resources judiciously. . . . Broken pens and parched throats obviously do not develop one at a time in an orderly fashion. . . . Closely related to the job of doling out material resources is that of granting special privileges to deserving students. In elementary classrooms it is usually the teacher who assigns coveted duties, such as serving on the safety patrol, or [doing errands for the teacher]. . . . A fourth responsibility of the teacher is that of serving as an official timekeeper. In many schools he is assisted in this job by elaborate systems of bells and buzzers. But even when the school day is mechanically punctuated by clangs and hums, the teacher is not entirely relieved of his responsibility.[10]

Jackson further points out that this "beehive of activity" is necessitated by the "crowded condition" of the classroom. It is the "press of numbers and of time that keeps the teacher so busy."[11]

As if the realities of classrooms were not enough, institutional constraints further limit the teacher's time for reflection. Teachers are rarely granted released time for reflection. There is continual pressure to cover a specified curriculum and to ensure that a highly diverse group of children—who attend school by compulsion rather than voluntarily—attain at least a minimal level of achievement.

Jackson (among others) argues that, given these conditions, there is no time for reflection and that reflection, if attempted, would only lead to paralysis of action and therefore less effective response to immediate circumstances.[12]

> The immediacy of classroom life, the fleeting and sometimes cryptic signs on which the teacher relies for determining his pedagogical moves and for evaluating the effectiveness of his actions calls into question the appropriateness of using conventional models of rationality to depict the teacher's classroom behavior when a teacher is standing before his students. . . . The spontaneity, immediacy and irrationality of the teacher's behavior seems to be its most salient characteristics. At such times there appears to be a high degree of uncertainty, unpredictability, and even confusion about the events in the classroom.[13]

But Jackson is also careful to point out another aspect of teaching:

> The fact that the teacher does not appear to be very analytic or deliberative in his moment-to-moment dealings with students should not obscure the fact that there are times when this is not true. During periods of solitude, in particular, before and after his face-to-face encounter with students, the teacher often seems to be engaged in a type of intellectual activity that has many of the formal properties of a problem-solving procedure. At such moments the teacher's work does look highly rational.
>
> This brief mention of the teacher's behavior during moments when he is not actively engaged with students calls attention to an important division in the total set of teaching responsibilities. There is a crucial difference it would seem between what the teacher does when he is alone at his desk and what he does when his room fills up with students.[14]

Research is increasingly confirming the belief that the quality of teacher planning outside the classroom (what Jackson terms the "preactive" phase of teaching) influences the quality of teaching within the classroom (what Jackson terms the "interactive" phase).[15]

Furthermore, despite the time constraints of classroom life, a certain degree of reflection is still even possible in the "interactive" phase of teaching. There are always lulls in the action, and even the fast pace of teaching requires some self-evaluation. It is at these times that the teacher is able to find the time in the classroom to reflect on what has been occurring and what is about to occur. If it were not for this reflection, the teacher would always be in a reactive rather than proactive posture.

To consider only the extremes of too much thought and blind action is to limit our options. Clearly, there needs to be a balance between thought and action.

What's the Point?   Some people argue that there is little point in reflecting on goals and practices when all the teacher does is implement someone else's ideas. They contend that "teachers are basically functionaries within a bureaucratic system; they have prescribed roles and responsibilities and in order to survive in that system they must always give way to institutional demands."[16] Furthermore, some claim, teachers inevitably conform to the norms of the school, which "washes out" any reflectiveness left over from preservice training.[17]

Although it is true that schools do socialize new teachers into a dominant "teacher culture," there is a wide range of viewpoints represented in that culture.[18] Teachers within the same school vary widely in evaluation and classroom management practices, goals, political beliefs, treatment of special pupils, adherence to textbooks, and friendliness versus businesslike roles. Surely, there is ample room for teachers to exercise individuality in teaching while working within the constraints of schools.

As with our discussion of time, there are two extremes on this issue. According to one view, every teacher is an individual, a person who is free to implement an educational philosophy by teaching what and how he or she wishes. Counter to this sociologically naive view is the position that the forces of bureaucratic socialization in schools are strong and efficient.[19] As with most other extreme views, there exists a more moderate position. This view asserts the "constant interplay between choice and constraint" in teaching.[20] As professionals working within a powerful institution, teachers have the opportunity to shape their identity, to take a stand even when they are in conflict with others, and to question common practices. Yes, teachers do implement someone else's ideas, but there is always room for personal judgment, decision, and criticism.

Psychological research supports this view. In contrast to both a behavioristic view (see B. F. Skinner's *Beyond Freedom and Dignity*) that a person's behavior is totally shaped by the environment and a humanistic view (see Carl Rogers's *Freedom to Learn in the 1980s*) that a person is free to respond as he or she chooses, a cognitive view stresses the interplay between the individual and the environment. In particular, this view suggests that the individual monitors his or her own actions and thought processes and actively makes decisions about what, and even how, to think.

Psychologists term this latter aspect of mental activity *metacognition*,[21] which simply means thinking about thinking. Metacognition in teaching includes the ability of teachers to monitor their cognitive processes, including understanding their own concepts, theories, and beliefs about teaching, learning, and their subject matter. Metacognition also includes controlling the decisions they make about what and how they teach.[22] In a sense, metacognition is a psychological approach to reflective teaching.

Is Reflection Really Necessary?   Many claim that reflection is not necessary for teaching. Intuition, they argue, is more important for effective teaching than careful analytic thought. In fact, some of the very best teachers do not seem to spend time reflecting on their work.

Much of this argument, and my response to it, follows the earlier discussion of time available for reflection. But there is more: Anybody who has tried to persuade a group of teachers to implement a particular curriculum has remarked at the degree to which teachers *adapt* rather than *adopt* curricula. Some curriculum developers have even gone to the extreme of attempting (in vain) to produce so-called teacher-proof curricula, an effort I view as an affront to the profession of teaching. That such attempts have been generally unsuccessful seems to be sufficient evidence that teachers are very selective about what they will incorporate into their classrooms. Teachers work within a practicality ethic that subjects any innovation to a test of cost versus benefit, feasibility, and consistency within the teachers' perceptions of themselves and their situations.[23] It is no wonder, then, that most innovations are "blunted on the classroom door."[24] The view of teachers that emerges from studies of curriculum implementation is one of active professionals constantly making educational decisions for their particular classrooms.

Once again, the two extremes are unworkable. Teachers operate neither on pure intuition nor on pure rational analysis. Teachers neither blindly adopt the materials and methods developed by "experts," nor insist on reinventing the wheel. Instead, teachers (especially effective ones) balance intuitive and reflective thought, using any resources they can find and adapting materials to suit their own purposes and methods.

How Do I Become More Reflective?

As mentioned earlier, there are two principal means used to help you reflect on your field experience: in-text questions/exercises and logs. You will find questions and exercises designed to encourage reflective thought throughout the text. If you take these questions and exercises seriously, you will find yourself engaged in an inquiry about teaching that ultimately requires a degree of self-analysis and appraisal. The questions and exercises will lead you to develop a sense of approach to your teaching, a perspective that will help you define your professional identity. If you pursue a career in teaching and continue to reflect on your professional experience, then your perspective will change over the years. These changes will constitute an important aspect of professional growth.

But, because different situations require different perspectives, there is a danger in making vague generalizations about teaching. You need a way to focus a perspective on specific field experiences rather than on teaching in general. Your daily or weekly logs will help you use your field experience as a specific reference point for your perspective. When you finish this field experience, you probably will not have developed a comprehensive framework for all of education, but most likely, you will have determined where you stand and what you believe in with regard to your specific situation. This will be no small accomplishment!

Daily or weekly logs, journals, or some other such method for recording events and personal reactions is one widely used method. Although somewhat time-consuming, written records and analyses provide a unique opportunity to keep track of events and to reflect privately on the personal and public meaning of those events. What happened? Why did it happen? What was my role? What beliefs did my actions reflect? Did my actions reflect beliefs and assumptions about which I was not aware? Did the consequences of my actions raise doubts or reinforce my beliefs? How should I act in the future on the basis of what happened?

When Should I Write My Logs?

A memory is most reliable if you write it down soon after the experience. Therefore, the longer you wait to jot down what happened, the less likely you are to remember the details accurately. A full description is not necessary at this point. However, if you intend to include quotations or detailed sequences of events, find a few minutes as soon as possible after an experience to note these details. This is not the time to reflect on the experience. Actually, if you allow some time to pass before you analyze the experience, you may gain insight and write a more thoughtful analysis.

The person who supervises your field experience may have a preferred or required format for your log or journal. Obviously, if this is the case, you should follow it. However, if you have a relatively free hand in terms of format, you can consider using the approach described in the following section.

What Is the Anatomy of a Log?

A lesson seeming unproblematic or even uneventful does not mean that there is nothing to observe. The essence of observation is the creation of insight out of what might seem to be routine and commonplace. Hidden beneath the surface of this lesson are unresolved issues that, when made visible, reveal possible alternative beliefs, values, and practice.[25]

It does not matter if we call it a log or a journal. What does matter is taking the opportunity to think about field experiences. It is difficult to think deeply about all our experiences. Therefore, I suggest a format that helps to focus thoughts on particularly significant events. Focusing on one or two events does not mean ignoring all others. Instead, it means keeping a record of all events while selecting, elaborating, and analyzing one or two that represent an important development in perspective, goals, or plans. Thus, the following format is designed to help you grow as a teacher by enabling you to benefit from your field experiences.

Fieldwork Log Format

A. Heading.   Name: (This is unnecessary if you keep your logs in a bound notebook.)
Date of field experiences reported: (A log entry should cover only one day and should be written the day of the experience. Otherwise, memories tend to fade.)
Time spent: (e.g., 1:30–3:00 P.M.)

B. Sequence of Events.   Make a brief list, describing what happened. By making a list, you keep a record of what happened. This record may be useful for future reference. It allows you to mention all events, even those that seemed insignificant at the time.

C. Elaboration of One or Two Significant Episodes.   An episode is an "event or sequence of events complete in itself but forming part of a larger one."[26] Select one or two episodes that are significant to you. An episode may be significant because what happened bothers you, excites you, causes you to rethink your initial ideas (e.g., your perspective, goals, or plans), or convinces you that your initial ideas were valid. Therefore, whether the episodes reflect your successes or your failures, they are significant if you learned something important from them.

Once you have selected one or two significant episodes, you should describe them in detail. When you describe an episode, try to relive it. Reliving the experience will enable you to provide as much detail as possible. Make certain that you include what people said, what they did, and how they looked. Try to be as specific as possible, including word-for-word quotations, as best you can remember. Recall what we said earlier about jotting notes as soon as possible. This type of description will provide you with material for reflection in the next section of the log.

Good descriptions should address all four common features (see Chapter 1), or at least you should have considered each. There is a tendency to provide descriptions that are too narrow, focusing only on what the teacher did or said. What we are looking for is a more complete description. Regarding subject matter, if the learner is working on a math problem, include the problem itself in this section. If not, at least describe the content of the "lesson" and the materials with which the learner is working. Regarding the learners, describe what they are saying and doing. Regarding the context, describe the surroundings including any relevant features, such as possible distractions or factors that may contribute to or detract from the teaching atmosphere.

In this description, try to avoid inferences about how people felt or what they thought (including your own feelings and thoughts). Save these inferences for your analysis.

D. Analysis of Episode(s).   An analysis of episodes includes an interpretation of what feelings and thoughts may have caused the episodes to occur, why they were significant, what questions they raise, and what you think you learned from them.

Try to figure out what you accomplished, identify problems that emerge and how you plan to follow up, and distill from the episodes what you learned. This last point is the most important. You may have learned what does and does not work in this situation. If so, describe what you conclude. But you may also have learned something about your philosophy of teaching (your perspective). Does the episode confirm your ideas or force you to reconsider them? Maybe some initial ideas you held rather dogmatically depend, to a large extent, on the situation in which you apply them. If so, what was it about the situation that affected the applicability of the ideas? Perhaps, the episode relates to something you read or learned about in this or some other education course. This would be the place to discuss it. In addition to describing how you felt, you should use the analysis section to discuss what you can say about yourself as a teacher and/or about teaching in general as a result of the experience. Many experiences raise more questions than they answer. You might use your logs as an opportunity to note questions arising during your field experiences that you want to discuss with your supervisor or bring up at a field experience seminar.

This suggested format requires you to distinguish between description and analysis, each with its own section of the log. When students begin writing logs, they typically have difficulty distinguishing between these two sections. When they do, they run the risk of undermining the use of their logs for reflection. Some problems include:

1. They add so much analysis to their "Episode" section that they neglect a full description of the episode. Or, they add so much description of episodes to their "Analysis" section that they never get a chance to analyze the episode.
2. They make unexamined assumptions in the "Episode" section without giving themselves the opportunity to reflect on those assumptions critically.

Note: Log writing in many ways resembles the data-collection method used by many qualitative researcher practitioners. In research with human subjects, it is imperative to protect the confidence, trust, and safety of the subjects. Therefore, anonymity is required.[27] In responsible research, many steps are taken to conceal the identity of the subjects; so in your logs, you should at the very least use pseudonyms when referring to individuals.

Criteria for Evaluating Fieldwork Logs

When I read students' logs, I use the following criteria in evaluating them:

1. Are all the *parts* there?
   a. Heading
   b. Sequence of events
   c. Episode
   d. Analysis
2. Episode description
   a. Are all *four common features* noted? Learners (what they said and did), Cooperating Teacher (when appropriate), Subject Matter (content of the lesson), Context (surroundings).
   b. Is it *detailed*? Use of quotes, rich description.
   c. Does it *stick to description* (note taking) rather than confounding description with *analysis* (note making).[28] Look especially for instances where the writer attributes (a) a particular motivation (e.g., "trying to please"), (b) a trait (e.g., "lazy"), (c) capabilities (e.g., "a good reader"), or emotional states (e.g., "angry") to the learners.
3. Analysis
   a. Does the analysis *focus on the episode described* earlier (rather than adding additional episode descriptions)?
   b. Does the analysis go beyond simply describing how the writer felt about the experience to include *why* he or she felt that way?
   c. Does the analysis include any *conclusions* from the experience? Conclusions may be in the form of questions that the writer is left with, or dilemmas that the writer realizes, rather than just hard-and-fast principles.
   d. Does the analysis draw on past experiences, readings, or exercises from teacher *education coursework*?
   e. Does the analysis lead to any *plans*? Will the writer do something as a consequence of this experience the next time he or she teaches?

Keep in mind that these are only guidelines; they should not be considered a formula for writing logs. Every teaching situation is different.

By reading some actual logs written by my students, you may get a clearer idea of how a log looks and what you might include in your own. For this reason, sample logs are included in Appendix B.

Toby Fulwiler's Introduction to *The Journal Book* is an especially useful resource on using logs for reflection.[29]

NOTES

1. John Dewey, *How We Think: A Restatement of the Relation of Reflective Thinking to the Educative Process* (Boston: D.C. Heath, 1933), p. 3.
2. Ibid., p. 17.

3. Ibid.
4. Carl Grant and Kenneth Zeichner, "On Becoming a Reflective Teacher," in *Preparing for Reflective Teaching*, ed. Carl A. Grant (Boston: Allyn & Bacon, 1984), p. 4.
5. Ibid.
6. D. John McIntyre, David Byrd, and Susan Foxx, "Field and Laboratory Experience," in *Handbook of Research on Teacher Education*, 2nd ed., ed. John Sikula (New York: Macmillan, 1996).
7. Donald Schon, *The Reflective Practitioner* (New York: Basic Books, 1983), p. 129.
8. I am indebted to Grant and Zeichner (ibid.) for the main points of this section.
9. Philip Jackson, *Life in Classrooms* (New York: Holt, Rinehart and Winston, 1968).
10. Ibid., pp. 11–12.
11. Ibid., p. 13.
12. Grant and Zeichner, "On Becoming a Reflective Teacher," in *Preparing for Reflective Teaching*, ed. Carl A. Grant (Boston: Allyn & Bacon, 1984), p. 9
13. Philip Jackson, *Life in Classrooms* (New York: Holt, Rinehart and Winston, 1968), pp. 151–152.
14. Ibid., p. 151.
15. Christopher Clark and Penelope Peterson, "Teachers' Thought Processes," in *Handbook of Research on Teaching*, 3rd ed., ed. Merlin Wittrock (New York: Macmillan, 1986), chapter 9.
16. Grant and Zeichner, "On Becoming a Reflective Teacher," in *Preparing for Reflective Teaching*, ed. Carl A. Grant (Boston: Allyn & Bacon, 1984), p. 10.
17. Ibid.
18. Ibid., p. 11.
19. Wayne Hoy and William Rees, "The Bureaucratic Socialization of Student Teachers," *Journal of Teacher Education* 28 (January–February 1977), 23–26.
20. Ibid., p. 11.
21. John Bransford, *Human Cognition* (Belmont, CA: Wadsworth, 1979), pp. 194–203.
22. Timothy Perfect and Bennet Schwartz, *Applied Metacognition* (Cambridge, UK: CUP, 2002), p. 4
23. Walter Doyle and Gerald Ponder, "The Ethic of Practicality: Implications for Curriculum Development," in *Curriculum Theory*, eds. Alex Molnar and John Zahorik (Washington, DC: Association for Supervision and Curriculum Development, 1977).
24. John Goodlad and Frances Klein, *Behind the Classroom Door* (Washington, DC: OH Jones, 1970).
25. Rob Walker and Clem Adelman, *A Guide to Classroom Observation* (London: Methuen, 1975), p. 18.
26. *Webster's New World Dictionary of the American Language*, 2nd college ed. (Englewood Cliffs, NJ: Prentice Hall, 1970), p. 471.
27. Family Life Development Center, *Depositing Data with the National Data Archive on Child Abuse and Neglect* (Ithaca, NY: Cornell University, 2002).
28. Carolyn Frank, *Ethnographic Eyes: A Teacher's Guide to Classroom Observation* (Portsmouth, NH: Heinemann, 1999), pp. 5–7.
29. Toby Fulwiler, ed., *The Journal Book* (Portsmouth, NH: Heinemann, 1987).

PART TWO

What Do You Bring to the Experience?

CHAPTER 4

Personal Influences on a Perspective

No one's mind is empty. This statement of the obvious applies to both novices and experts. We have ideas and ideals about such things as parenting, marriage, coaching, and appropriate bedside manner, even though we may never have officially been a parent, spouse, coach, or doctor. The same can be said of teaching. We all have some beliefs about what good teaching is, regardless of whether we have official status as a teacher.

Our own beliefs, principles, and ideals (termed *perspective*), however unexamined or incomplete they may now be, function for each of us as a personal platform. They justify and unify our decisions and actions (just as a political platform does). A personal platform is what we stand for and what we stand on.[1]

A perspective also functions as a lens through which we look at the world of teaching. As a lens, a perspective affects our perception and interpretation of teaching. It does this by forming expectations of what we will experience (the *what* question), by helping us to understand basic reasons for the nature of the experience (the *why* question), and by offering standards for judging the quality of the experience (the *how well* question). Although some distortion is inevitable with any lens, without one, we would see only what William James called "bloomin', buzzin' confusion." By becoming aware of the perspective with which we operate, we can at least become sensitive to the bases for our own approach to teaching and at best become capable of changing our approach as we gain both new ideas and new teaching experiences. The primary goal of this chapter is to help you begin thinking about your own perspective on teaching; this thinking will make your perspective more explicit and thereby help to clarify it and reconsider its validity. Your teaching perspective is the constellation of assumptions, beliefs, and intentions that guide and justify your actions in the classroom. The five most common perspectives on teaching held by teachers are described below. Each perspective uses a distinctive lens through which to view acquisition of knowledge, learning, and strategies for teaching.[2]

1. *Transmission perspective.* Teachers with this perspective are committed to ensuring that students master content. Learning takes place by adding more and more content but being careful not to overload students with too much information. The teacher must provide clear objectives, set high standards, deliver detailed and structured lectures, clarify misunderstandings, and use valid assessments to successfully transmit knowledge to students.

2. *Development perspective.* Teachers with this perspective are committed to meeting students where they are and then helping to develop reasoning and problem-solving skills. Emphasis is placed on changing the ways students think rather than increasing the amount of information they know. Using a constructivist approach, a teacher allows learners to construct understanding of material instead

of making them reproduce the teacher's understanding. This perspective relies on the use of questions, problems, and case studies to move students from less to more sophisticated ways of reasoning.

3. *Apprenticeship perspective.*   Teachers with this perspective are committed to initiating learners into an educational community of practice. This includes helping students identify themselves as being members of the learning community. To learn, individuals must have competence in a discipline and see themselves as learners in training. Teachers use scaffolding techniques in order to break complex information into simpler pieces that are easier to learn. This perspective uses real tasks to facilitate learning—similar to an apprentice working in a shop to master the skills necessary to be competent.

4. *Nurturing perspective.*   Teachers with this perspective are committed to providing encouragement, support, clear expectations, and appropriate goals. Teachers believe that affect is the most important component of learning. Students are motivated to learn when they perceive that they are in a safe environment. Teachers need to develop an ethos of trust among peers, as well as an atmosphere of trust and care while providing a challenging curriculum. Learning happens when teachers and students communicate and respond to emotional and intellectual needs.

5. *Social reform perspective.*   Teachers with this perspective are committed to creating social change. Learning must be linked to ideals necessary to create a better society. Teachers believe that the ideals they are committed to are appropriate for all learners. They are dedicated to exposing learners to diversity and encourage students to critically reflect on the status quo and their own previously held assumptions. During the educational process, the dignity of the learners is always paramount.

The vast majority (90 percent) of teachers combine one or two perspectives in their teaching lives.[3] Where do perspectives come from? To be frank, the answer has me puzzled. Clearly, past experience helps to shape perspective. This chapter represents an attempt to help you understand the role of your past experiences in forming your present beliefs about teaching. Admittedly, I do not fully understand why some experiences have more impact than others or why different people experience the same set of events differently. But even without understanding the nature of human experience and its relation to perspectives, it is safe to claim that past experience is significant and that thinking about past experiences can contribute to the identification and examination of current perspectives on teaching.

This chapter will be the first step in the initial formulation of your own perspective. There will be no "correct" answers to any of the exercises. Instead, they are intended to guide your thinking about your own approach to teaching, your own beliefs, ideals, commitments, principles, and values. In doing the exercises, you will examine two kinds of teaching-related experiences you have already had: your extensive experience as a learner and your (limited, mostly informal) experience as a teacher.

Experience as a Learner

> Those who cannot remember the past not only relive it; they tend to impose it, mistakes and all, on others.[4]

Not all learning is accompanied by teaching. In fact, some of our most potent learning experiences take place in the absence of any "teachers" (in both the formal and informal senses). There is no doubt, however, that much learning depends on effective teaching. We can examine our beliefs on learning and teaching by thinking about our own past experience as learners.

EXERCISE 4.1

Significant Learning Experiences

You might try to think about some potent learning experiences you have had. To do this, consider all experiences in which you learned something significant, something that has stayed with you. A comprehensive list of settings is impossible, but let me try to help jog your memory. Consider the following contexts and people:

- *Schools*—teachers in and out of classrooms, coaches, or extracurricular activities
- *At home*—your parents, siblings, grandparents, and other relatives
- *Chance meetings*—for example, people met while traveling
- *Religious groups or events*—Sunday school, religious services, talks with religious leaders
- *Workplaces*—bosses, co-workers, customers
- *Libraries*—school projects, pursuing a personal interest, browsing
- *Music instruction*—classes, self-instruction, informal teachers
- *Friendships*—peers, friends much older or much younger than you
- *Counseling*—for example, psychological, legal, or drug counselors
- *Health related*—for example, doctors and nurses

Spend 5 or 10 minutes writing down the three most potent and significant learning experiences you can recall. Each experience should have had relatively discrete duration—that is, a time during which you were learning something important to you.

▶

When I have asked my students to do this exercise, typically they have mentioned one of their college teachers; one of their elementary or secondary school teachers; one of their family members, especially their mother or father; a nonschool music or sports teacher; or a close friend. For many of my students, the significant learning experiences involve no teacher. The conditions for a powerful learning experience are apparently set by such factors as the intensity of the situation, the person's own emotional state, and being on one's own. For example, many students mention their first year in college or the death of a friend, relative, or pet as a powerful learning experience.

What follows is the work of three students who were asked to do this exercise. Perhaps, reading their work will help you to see what types of experiences qualify and how to describe them.

Student Response 1

Taking a course in critical thinking and analytical writing during my first semester in college. The classroom setting was not crucial to the learning experience, and most of the learning was done by working on essays. The experience was special to me in that I felt I had created something unique, a product of my own thinking that no one could have constructed in the same way. At the time, I was eager to learn this subject and to learn if I could make it in college at all.

The sudden death of a close friend in my hometown. I learned how close death can really be and that no loved one should be taken for granted. The setting was crucial to the experience in that I attended the funeral and Mass and saw how others experienced it also. The learning

(continued)

was personal in that the person involved meant a lot to me. I needed to learn why I felt the way I did about his dying, searching for reasons for these feelings.

The setting was my home when I took up the hobby of silent motion picture collecting and reading. I absorbed a tremendous amount of information on the subject which, even thirteen years later, comes easily to mind. At the time (1969), I was one year shy of draft eligibility and consciously interested in learning about other, better times.

Student Response 2

The three most potent learning experiences were *learning sign language, learning how to be a better friend,* and *learning about my father's World War II experiences.*

I learned sign language in a classroom situation and from working with hearing-impaired students. This learning experience would be considered to be "subject matter." It is also a way of getting to know hearing-impaired people and helping them to get along better. I felt a strong need to learn so that I could communicate with the students on the only level they know.

Learning how to be a better friend sounds vague and also like something that would take a lifetime. A very special friend gave me a crash course *just* by being my friend. She taught me a lot about myself. She taught me how to be a listener, how to be understanding and giving, and how to be less selfish.

Learning about my father's WW II experiences was very important to me because not only did I learn about his life, I learned that he can be very open, given the opportunity. I learned from him while driving from Cornell to my home. I'll always cherish the experience because it was the first time in my life my father actually told me about something very emotional and important to him.

Student Response 3

My first potent learning experience occurred when I was taking piano lessons from a blind man who was teaching me to play songs by ear. Usually, I would tell him that I wanted to learn a certain song I heard on the radio, and he would play it on the piano while taping what he was playing. I would take the tape home and learn the song. Finally, one day I asked him to teach me a certain song, and he told me to buy the single and learn it myself (without him as an intermediate step). I did this and was successful. I no longer needed his help to take what I was hearing (many different instruments) and play it on the piano. This was important because it set the stage for my future as a musician—playing by ear is sometimes very convenient. It also helped me to write my own music, indirectly.

Another experience was when I learned the quantum theory of the elements. I was having a difficult time grasping it and was feeling frustrated and stupid. A teacher of mine kept patiently explaining it to me, and when it finally became clear, I felt like shouting "Eureka!" through the halls of the school.

A third experience was when I learned to windsurf. This was important to me because I'm not very athletic, and I felt like I was broadening my horizons. I had a teacher who imparted the basic knowledge, but I learned mostly by practicing with this knowledge in mind (got very wet in the process!). When I finally got the hang of it, I was very proud because others were trying it too—some not as successfully—and I sort of made it look easy!

Next, you might profit from analyzing your three learning experiences. For example, try to identify and write down why each was potent for you. You might warm up for this analysis by first trying it on the three sample responses you have just read. What elements made each experience significant? Consider the following:

- *Context.* In what setting did each experience occur? In a classroom or elsewhere? Was the setting crucial to the experience?

- *Teacher.* Who was involved? Were you alone or with others? Did a "teacher" bring about an experience, did you do it, or did it happen spontaneously?

▶

- *Subject matter.* Was there anything special about what you learned? Did the learning fall under the rubric of "subject matter," or was the learning more unusual and/or personal?

▶

- *Learner.* Was there anything unique about you at the time of each experience? For example, did you feel an especially strong need to learn?

▶

Next, try to draw generalizations about the conditions under which you learn best. Do you find any similarities, or was each experience and learning process unique?

▶

When I have asked undergraduate students to do this exercise, roughly half of the learning experiences have turned out to be instances of either learning without a teacher or learning with a nonschool teacher. Clearly, students bring to our classrooms things they have learned outside classrooms as well as inside other classrooms. We all know this fact, but we all seem to forget it periodically.

On the basis of this exercise, consider your uniqueness as a learner and how this might affect your teaching. How have your past learning experiences affected your views on teaching? For example, as a consequence of your experiences, how important is it for teaching to involve the following?

- A close relationship with the teacher
- Being intrinsically motivated to learn
- Learning nonacademic subject matter
- Intense emotion surrounding the learning experience
- A feeling of competence or success by the learner

If your past learning experiences have strongly affected your views, consider the validity of generalizing the conditions under which *you* learn best to conditions of learning for others. In particular, consider the limitations imposed by classroom teaching on providing the conditions required for your most significant learning experiences. Which of your conclusions are generalizable to most public school classroom teaching?

▶

Now we look more specifically at your past classroom teachers, because it is likely that they have contributed a great deal to your conceptions about teaching.[5] It is experiences with past classroom teachers that constitute what Dan Lortie[6] describes as the 13,000-hour "apprenticeship by observation" that people experience before they even reach college.

EXERCISE 4.2

Most Successful and Unsuccessful Teachers

Try to think back over your 13 to 16 years of elementary, secondary, and higher education. Try to identify the two or three most unsuccessful teachers you can remember. Write their names or some identifying characteristics, if you cannot remember their names. Now jot down next to each what made that person so unforgettable. Do you think most of his or her other students would agree with you, or was your response to this teacher somewhat special? Was this teacher successful with any students? If so, what made them different from you? What was the subject matter? Was this a factor in your response? Were there special circumstances with regard to community, the school, the class, the teacher's personal life, or your own state of mind? Would you find this teacher just as intolerable today?

▶

Now try to think of the two or three most successful teachers you have ever had. Jot their names down or write something down to identify each of them. What made each of them so successful? What did each of them teach? Was the subject matter a factor in each teacher's success? Do you think other students responded to these teachers as favorably as you? Who might disagree, and how were these students different from you? Were there any special circumstances, such as a new and exciting curriculum or special events occurring in the school, community, or world (e.g., space shots, book censorships, a science fair)? Would you find each of these teachers just as wonderful today?

▶

Look over your two lists and notes. What did the teachers do that made them successful or unsuccessful? What can you conclude about teaching?

▶

Experiences we have as learners are greatly affected by the lenses through which we view the world. These lenses are formed by many factors, some of which may be age, socio-economic status, religion, ethnicity, race, sexual orientation, and family background.

Our lenses are also formed in part by prevailing societal stereotypes (e.g., the belief that all poor people are irresponsible or that all rich children are spoiled) and by our experiences with particular individuals who are different from us. Although we may try hard to avoid stereotyping people, at an unconscious level, we may make judgments about people based on stereotypes. Whether they are conscious or unconscious, stereotypes are important to examine, because they may cause misunderstandings that lead to ineffective teaching and learning. It is quite likely that you will teach learners whose backgrounds are, at least in some way, different from yours. The unexamined assumptions and expectations you hold regarding these differences (many derived from stereotypes) may significantly affect your ability to reach your learners.

Take time now to examine how your background affects your perspective.

How might your beliefs about people of different ages, ethnic, or racial groups affect your teaching? Also examine your assumptions about people who hold different religious beliefs or have a different sexual orientation, or about people with physical, emotional, or mental disabilities.

▶

How might your views about people who live in locations (e.g., rural, urban, suburban) different from your own affect your teaching? Or how might your views about people who have a different family structure (e.g., stepparent, adopted children, single parent, same-sex parents) than yours affect your teaching?

▶

If you have an opportunity to do so, compare your conclusions with those of your present classmates. Discuss with them what makes your conclusions, and therefore your perspective on teaching, different from theirs. Consider the extent to which your school experiences have contributed to your views about teaching. To what extent have you examined these views? Often we operate from a set of assumptions that affect our expectations, judgments, and preferences of which we are not even aware. It is one thing to operate from a set of unexamined beliefs and another to hold onto those beliefs dogmatically in the face of contrary evidence. As long as we remain tentative about our beliefs and continually try to test them, we continue to grow.

Many of the beliefs we hold as teachers are derived from our experiences as students. In Appendix A, you will respond to a set of statements designed to help you identify your perspective on your field experience as a teacher (the Teacher Belief Inventory [TBI]). For now, we will focus on your perspective on being a student. In Appendix A, you will also find the Student Belief Inventory (SBI). Take the time to complete it now.

Favorite Subject Matter and Topics

It seemed impertinent when on my first day of teaching a student asked, "Why should anyone learn this stuff?" I had no answer, so I told the student to be quiet; he was, and the question remained unanswered. However, as the days wore on, the question nagged at me. It was, after all, a good question, no matter what the student's motive in asking it. We should know why we are taking people's time and consuming the community's resources for teaching particular topics in language arts, social studies, math, science, physical education, vocational education, foreign languages, computer science, home economics, industrial arts, and all the other subjects. At the very least, we ought to know why anyone should learn the particular subject matter and topics we teach.

What are your favorite subject matters? Are you most interested in fiction, poetry, biology, history, mathematics, sports, health, or some other subject matter?

▶

What specific topics interest you the most? Sports, ecology, gardening, music, travel, photography, history, poetry, or some other topics?

▶

EXERCISE 4.3

Most and Least Important Courses Taken

Think back over your schooling career. Try to identify the five courses or subjects you have studied that, in retrospect, seem most important. Do the same for those you consider least important. *Webster's New World Dictionary* defines *important* as "meaning a great deal; having much significance, consequence or value." The less important, the more trivial, time wasting, and fruitless.

(continued)

EXERCISE 4.3 Continued

FORM 4.3   Most and least important courses

Most important

1.

2.

3.

4.

5.

Least important

1.

2.

3.

4.

5.

When I try this exercise with large heterogeneous classes of undergraduates, I receive two lists that are almost identical. That is, every subject that someone considers most important someone else considers least important. My conclusion is that no subject will get universal support. A lot depends on the particular learner.

For each course you listed, examine your reasons for putting it in a particular column.

What criteria for selecting subject matter do your choices imply? Consider the following possibilities:[7]

- *Context.*   Are your choices based on their contribution to further learning (formal or nonformal), to your vocation, or to personal-social living? That is, are your choices based on *what* they are useful for?
- *Further learning.*   For choices that are related to further learning, are any important because they provide "basic tools" for further learning or because they offer fundamental ideas (i.e., key concepts or broadly applicable explanations)?
- *Vocation.*   For choices that are related to your vocation (or avocation), are any important because they contributed to selection, performance, or upgrading of your vocation/avocation?
- *Personal-social living.*   Are any of your choices based on their contribution to the society or community as a whole, while others are based on their contribution to you as an individual? That is, are your choices based on *who* (i.e., society or individual) is supposed to benefit from them?
- *Use situations.*   Are any of your choices based on the frequency or diversity of situations in which you put them to use or how crucial (though possibly rare or unique) the situation is when they are put to use? That is, are your choices based on their *situational usefulness*?
- *Timing.*   Are any of your choices important or unimportant because they are useful at the present time, in the foreseeable future, or in the remote future? That is, are your choices based on *when* they are useful?

- *Use mode.*   Do your choices reflect an emphasis on using knowledge to solve the types of problems and perform the kinds of skills similar to those taught (e.g., vocational training, reading), to provide ideas that enable you to interpret the social and natural world in which you live (e.g., physics), or to provide imagery and other associations that enrich experience (e.g., poetry)?

If these questions help you uncover some of the implicit reasons you value certain subject matter and topics over others, try jotting down these insights here.

▶

Many of these assumptions about education might underlie your justification for teaching particular topics. However, personal history plays a role also.

EXERCISE 4.4

The Road to My Favorite Subject Matter and Topics

Think back over your life, both in and out of school. Jot down significant events (e.g., a trip to Europe) or people (e.g., a brother-in-law who is a scientist) that have influenced the value you place on your favorite subject matter and topics. That is, what events and people have led to your special interests?

FORM 4.4   Key events and people

Events	People

Experience as a Teacher

In Chapter 1, you made an inventory of your prior teaching experiences (see Form 1.1). Now you can examine them as sources of your initial perspective on teaching.

EXERCISE 4.5

Analysis of Prior Teaching Experiences

For each of the prior teaching experiences you listed in Form 1.1 in Chapter 1, try to analyze the extent and the nature of your success. Remember, we are referring to nonformal teaching in addition to formal teaching. Form 4.5 may help you perform this analysis.

(continued)

EXERCISE 4.5 **Continued**

FORM 4.5 **Analysis of prior teaching experiences**

Description of experience (from Form 1.1 in Chapter 1)	Success rating (1 = failure) (5 = success)	Criteria for judging success	Factors in success or failure
1.			
2.			
3.			
4.			
5.			

Based on this analysis, what can you conclude about teaching? On what sorts of success criteria do you typically rely? To what extent do these criteria reflect your views about what is important in teaching? To what extent do these criteria depend on the teaching situations? Are you likely to use these criteria in your field experience?
▶

How successful have you been at teaching? To what extent has your success motivated you to pursue a career in teaching?
▶

What factors have contributed to your successes or failures? How likely is it that these factors will affect your success or failure during your field experience?
▶

To what extent and in what ways have your prior teaching experiences affected your beliefs about and ideals for teaching?
▶

EXERCISE 4.6

The Role of the Media on Beliefs

In addition to the highly personal influences on your beliefs about teaching that we have probed in this chapter, there are also other influences. The next two chapters explore some of these. However, in preparation for those two chapters, consider the role of the media in your beliefs. Think back now about books and magazine articles you may have read and TV programs and movies you may have viewed. Jot down (in the space provided or on a separate sheet of paper) titles, authors, or subjects of pieces of work, as best you can remember them, that have had an impact on your thinking about teaching.

EXERCISE 4.6 Continued

What I remember about it	Impact on my thinking
Books	
Articles	
TV programs	
Movies	

NOTES

1. Decker Walker, *Fundamentals of Curriculum* (New York: Harcourt Brace Jovanovich, 1990).
2. Daniel Pratt, "Good Teaching: One Size Fits All?" in *Contemporary Viewpoints on Teaching Adults Effectively*, ed. Jovita Ross-Gordon (San Francisco: Jossey-Bass, 2002), p. 7
3. Ibid.
4. Eliot Wigginton, *The Foxfire Book* (Garden City, NY: Anchor Books, 1972), p. 10.
5. Virginia Richardson, "The Role of Attitudes and Beliefs in Learning to Teach," in *Handbook of Research on Teacher Education*, 2nd ed., ed. John Sikula (New York: Macmillan, 1996).
6. Dan Lortie, *Schoolteacher* (Chicago: University of Chicago Press, 1975).
7. Mauritz Johnson, *Intentionality in Education* (Albany, NY: Center for Curriculum Research and Services, 1977), pp. 134–135.

CHAPTER 5

Contributions of Foundational Studies

Many teacher-educators believe that a person's perspective on teaching is formed by more than the experiences that the person has had as learner and teacher. They cite the importance of concepts and theories drawn from certain disciplines. After all, they claim, teaching implies helping a student learn things, which, in turn, contributes to the achievement of broader educational aims. Appropriate aims are, at least in part, a *philosophical* issue, and the nature of learning is a *psychological* issue. In addition, teachers and students operate in one of our society's most significant institutions and therefore teachers must take into account the *sociology* of teaching. Awareness of these aspects of teaching leads teacher-educators to consider philosophy, psychology, and sociology as three of the "foundations" of teaching. Other foundational studies include the history, economics, and politics of teaching.[1] Most preservice teacher education programs, therefore, require some coursework in at least two or three of these disciplines.

For foundational studies to be useful to field experiences, we must find ways of using foundational studies to help us think about and thereby enrich these experiences. One way that the foundations can do this is by supplying concepts for interpreting a particular field experience. For example, philosophy offers concepts such as the scientific methods, autonomy, and structures of knowledge; psychology offers concepts such as feedback, transfer, and intrinsic motivation; and sociology offers concepts such as role, bureaucracy, socialization, socioeconomic status (SES), and subculture. If these concepts help us to understand what is going on in a school or in a classroom, then they may be considered useful for the analysis.

Another way to understand the contributions of the foundations is to view them as a source of questions and issues that must be addressed by any thoughtful teacher. For instance, philosophy, among other things, raises questions about the purposes to which teachers should give highest priority—transmission of our cultural heritage, citizenship, self-fulfillment, or vocational development; psychology, among other things, raises questions regarding the effectiveness of competition for improving motivation; and sociology raises questions about such things as the kinds of values, norms, and social definitions implicitly taught through the rules, procedures, and grading practices established by the school and the teacher.

The purpose of this chapter is to help you use your foundational studies as bases for reflection about your field experiences. Although your perspective on teaching could embody a wide range of possible issues, the six issues we discuss encompass many (but not all) dimensions of most teachers' perspectives. We will examine each issue as a possible dimension of your perspective on teaching and in order to identify concepts you might find useful for thinking about it. We will also analyze some possible positions on the issue in order to help you clarify your own position.

The issues we will examine are control, learning and motivation, pupil diversity, knowledge, the teacher's role, and the relation between school and society. These same six issues are used to organize the teacher interview questions in Chapter 11 and the belief inventories in Appendix A.

These six issues can be expressed as questions that a teacher's perspective might address.

Six Basic Issues of Teaching

1. *Control.* Who should control what goes on in teaching, and what should be the range of their control?
2. *Learning.* How do people learn in terms of both the process of learning and the motivation for it?
3. *Diversity.* How unique are learners and how should one treat learners on the basis of their differences?
4. *Knowledge.* What is knowledge? Is knowledge a given set of facts, concepts, and generalizations to be transmitted, or is it more a personal or social construction developed by processes of reasoning and negotiation?
5. *Role.* How formal (versus personal) should teachers be in their relationships with the learners?
6. *School and society.* To what extent do the sources of and solutions to teachers' problems require structural changes in schools or society?

Taken as a whole, the six basic issues cover a broad range.[2] We can see this scope by locating each issue on our earlier map of four common features (refer to Figure 1.1). The issues of student diversity and how students learn clearly center on the *learners.* The teacher's role is obviously an issue centering on the *teacher* and how he or she relates to the learners. School and society issues can be considered primarily *contextual* issues in teaching. Issues regarding the nature of knowledge reflect a dominant concern for conceptions of the *subject matter* we teach. Issues of control cover all four common features.

Control

- "A teacher who cannot control the class cannot teach."
- "The most important lesson to be learned is respect for authority."
- "In a democratic society, the teacher should make all decisions democratically."

Maybe one or more of these common sayings reflect your own viewpoint on control. When we talk about control in teaching, we are concerned with issues of *who* controls *whom* and in *what areas* they should exert their control. The "who" and "whom" refer to teachers, students, parents, administrators, textbook publishers, and state education personnel, among others. "What areas" refers to the particular domains in which the teachers, students, and others might exert control. Issues of control include the following:

- Whether the teacher is merely an intermediary between the administration or textbook writers and the learner
- How strict the teacher should be
- How extensive the teacher's control is (as compared with that of the students, parents, administrators, etc.) in determining the amount of *time* spent on activities and the *rules* of conduct in the classroom (both the number and the kind of rules)
- Who should select and design classroom activities, the standards used to evaluate performance, and the goals of instruction
- How closely teachers must adhere to the school's goals and policies

Let us see what light we can expect foundation courses to shed on such questions of control. In an attempt to answer these questions, we will examine sociologically the teacher's rules and the socialization process as a means of controlling students and the curriculum as a means of controlling both teachers and students. First, let's examine a scenario that highlights several control issues.

Read the following scenario and think through your responses. Confer with others to see how they would handle this issue.

You have given students 20 minutes to read quietly. You have told them they are not to talk during this time. Two students begin whispering quietly. They read for a bit and then whisper again. Other students do not seem to notice them. No one is bothered by the whispering, and no one else follows their lead—the other students keep reading.

Will you tell the two students to stop whispering? If so, why? Which issues are at stake for you—authority, rules, socialization? Does it matter if the two are whispering about the story they are reading? If a struggling student comes to you and begins asking questions about the reading, do you interact quietly? If so, are you breaking the rules?

Let us take a quick look at schools through the eyes of a sociologist. To most sociologists, the school and the classroom are social systems embedded within broader social systems, that is, the community, state, and nation. In any social system, there is bound to be conflict and, therefore, coercion.[3]

One conflict "exists between the bureaucratic authority of administrators, based on their position in a hierarchy of offices, and the professional authority of teachers, based on their training in a body of theory related to learning."[4] Another conflict derives from the compulsory nature of schooling, "which captures students for a prolonged period." This coercive situation drives students to "form their own subcultures, as a means of coping with the pervasive and systematic demands of school authorities." These subcultures increase the level of conflict, because they typically do not support the educational goals of the school's faculty and staff.

Rather than emphasize conflict, some sociologists point out that any social system to some extent depends on a "consensus" of values and beliefs, if that social system is to function.[5] The school attempts to achieve consensus by socializing students, that is, by teaching self-control, discipline, and respect for authority. Of all the beliefs and values the schools try to instill, some consensus theorists consider the most significant to be the belief that achievement is the basis for the allocation of people to occupational slots in the society.[6] However, other, more critical, sociologists claim that schools reward students not only on the basis of their achievement but also on the basis of their social class.[7] Diverse sociological ideas, stemming from these different sociological theories, provide different bases for thinking about questions of control.

Rules. For a sociologist, rules express norms of behavior. The methods of their enforcement are an expression of the sanctions the teacher chooses to employ. The enforcement of rules, then, is one means by which the teacher deals with the inevitable conflict arising within an autocratic form of governance.[8] Furthermore, the rules teachers enforce reflect the type of socialization process that the school promotes.[9]

Consider the following questions about rules:

What rules do you plan to make explicit to your class?

Should rules be made cooperatively with the class or should they be made only by the teacher?

Do you think you will expect students to follow any rules that you do not plan to state explicitly?

What will be the scope of both your explicit and implicit rules? That is, what will they cover?

Consider the following areas:

- Speaking order
- Movement within the classroom
- Movement outside the classroom
- Arrival time
- Seating posture
- Noise level
- Format and neatness of written work
- Dress
- Manners (student–teacher and student–student)

What sorts of sanctions do you think you might impose on students who break rules? What sorts of sanctions would you never impose?
▶

Socialization and the Hidden Curriculum.   Rules are explicit expressions of norms of behavior, but they are also the least effective form of regulation. Sociologists point out that schools prefer to have students follow norms of behavior without coercion. To the extent that the students internalize the school's norms, the need for rules decreases. Students who control themselves require few rules. In a sense, explicit rules cover only those areas for which socialization has been incomplete or ineffective.

You might want to consider the sorts of assumptions you make concerning socialization. For example, consider the sorts of norms you will expect students to follow in the absence of explicit rules.
▶

Often we base our expectations about student behavior on our own past experience. These expectations can lead to many surprises, however, if we happen to teach in a school with a student population much different from the schools we attended. Because the home is the basis for most of the socialization process, the more you know about the community, the better prepared you will be in dealing with your students. (See Chapter 8 for some suggestions on how to learn about the community.)

Think through your reactions to the following scenario, keeping in mind your expectations of students.

Students in your class suggest that they need to have an hour a week alone, without you in the room. They argue that a different level of comfort exists for some students when you are away. They would like to use this time to work collaboratively. They assure you that they will stay focused on schoolwork and not abuse the arrangement. How will you react? What might make you uncomfortable with this scenario? What conditions might you consider to accommodate the students' request? Remain in the hall outside the room, leave door open? What is the relationship between proximity and control?

Some educational sociologists consider the school's norms of behavior to be manifestations of what they call a "hidden curriculum."[10] They claim that the hidden curriculum is a powerful means of "social control." Included within the concept of a hidden curriculum are many outcomes that may result (and may even be expected to result) from the enforcement of both explicit and implicit rules. These potential outcomes may include docility; how to sit still for long periods under crowded conditions; a belief that effort, neatness, and promptness are more important than achievement; a belief that students get what they deserve in school; a belief that one's personality must be kept under constant control; a respect for authority; and many others. You will likely find some of these outcomes desirable, some undesirable, and some controversial. Actually, it depends on your own view of schools. Some people discover the hidden curriculum and exclaim, "Oh, my goodness!" whereas others proclaim, "Thank goodness!"

You might consider the kind of hidden curriculum you would like to discover in schools, the kind you suspect exists but hope does not exist, and what to do with a hidden curriculum when you find one.[11] Your preferred hidden curriculum is an expression of your preferred kinds of social control.

A closely related issue raised by sociologists concerns the hidden curricula of different SES groups. Not only may low-SES groups sometimes receive different official curricula, they may also receive different hidden curricula. Some sociologists examine the rules enforced by teachers in schools within different communities.[12] For example, they find that, in contrast to classrooms in high-SES communities, classrooms in low-SES communities restrict movement more within the class and outside the classroom (e.g., require bathroom passes), allow for less student decision making with regard to topics, allow less independent project work, require more busy work, and allow less student-to-student talk in the classroom.

Consider the ways in which the hidden curricula of low-SES classrooms might differ from those of high-SES classrooms. Contrast what low-SES students might learn with what high-SES students might learn as a consequence of the classroom norms. Would you as a teacher treat low-SES students differently from high-SES students? If not, what do you think accounts for the findings of sociologists? Maybe you are different from the teachers in the sociological studies just mentioned.

▶

The Curriculum as a Means of Control.   Norms may be the most obvious means of control, but plans also control. One type of plan is the curriculum. Whether a curriculum is conceived as a plan describing intended instructional methods (i.e., means), intended learning outcomes (i.e., ends), or both, it controls both the teacher and the student by legitimizing some types of content and activities and delegitimizing others.

The more bureaucratically organized the school, the further up the hierarchy important decisions are made. Yet the more teachers seek to professionalize their occupation, the more they want to make important decisions themselves. This conflict between teachers and administrators often centers on selection of textbooks, methods, and curriculum. Attempts to "standardize" the curriculum can be seen as attempts to further bureaucratize the school and, thus, to deprofessionalize teachers.

To what extent do you intend to follow the school's curriculum if you happen to disagree with it? To what extent do you believe you should "adjust your teaching to the administration's view of good teaching practice" and be "obedient, respectful, and loyal to the principal" regarding matters of curriculum?[13]

▶

A school's curriculum defines what is to count as "school knowledge," as opposed to "non-school everyday knowledge."[14] For sociologists such as Weber,[15] curricula are defined in terms of a dominant group's idea of the "educated person."

Some sociologists are concerned with how the imposition of certain knowledge (i.e., curricula) on lower-SES groups prevents these groups from thinking for themselves.[16] These sociologists suggest that the dominant group's "common sense" becomes legitimized by being labeled "school knowledge" (and by being made available to certain groups through the official curriculum), whereas other groups' common sense is ignored.

This sociological perspective goes a step further, to describe the sort of knowledge characterized as school knowledge and thereby is included in the school's curriculum. According to these sociologists, knowledge that serves "to legitimate a rigid hierarchy between teacher and taught"[17] is accorded the highest status. Such high-status knowledge is likely to manifest "a clear distinction between what is taken to count as knowledge, and what is not."[18] Furthermore, high-status knowledge is likely (1) to emphasize written rather than oral presentation, (2) to emphasize individual rather than group work in both instruction and evaluation, (3) to be abstract, and (4) to be "at odds with daily life and common experience."[19]

You might consider how you would characterize the subject matter you intend to teach according to this perspective:

- Its status
- The students to whom it will and will not be made available
- The likelihood that different curricula in this subject matter will be offered to different students (e.g., different "tracks")

Philosophical and Psychological Perspectives on Control. This analysis of control-related issues is certainly not exhaustive. For example, the sociological discussion of the teacher's enforcement of rules could have included psychologically based techniques for "managing" classrooms, such as behavior-modification techniques. The predominantly sociological discussion of the teacher's responsibilities for the official curriculum of the state or school could have included philosophical analyses of liberty and academic freedom, including an analysis of who is entitled to control what and for whom.[20] The sociological discussion of knowledge could have included a philosophical analysis of the educated person. It could also have included a psychological analysis of the likely transfer-of-learning (i.e., "generativeness") that different subjects offer or a theoretical account of the relation among knowledge, attitudes, and actions. These discussions only suggest the range of possible contributions to issues of control offered by philosophy, sociology, and psychology.

Learning and Motivation[21]

If you have ever taken an educational psychology course, then there is likely to be no doubt in your mind that questions regarding learning and motivation are based on psychological theory. Whether they discuss learning or motivation, educational psychology courses often contrast behaviorist and cognitive theories. Behaviorist accounts of learning provide concepts such as the following to describe learning and teaching:

- *Law of exercise.* Repetition of a conditioned response strengthens the bond between the stimulus situation and the response; that is, practice makes perfect
- *Reinforcement.* Anything that increases the strength of a behavior, with positive reinforcement using rewards and negative reinforcement using the withdrawal of unpleasant situations
- *Partial reinforcement.* Less than 100 percent reinforcement of responses
- *Operant conditioning.* Eliciting behaviors and then reinforcing them

- *Shaping.* Reinforcement of successive steps or approximations toward an ultimate target behavior
- *Modeling.* Providing a demonstration of a behavior for learners to observe and then to imitate
- *Self-pacing.* Pacing placed under learner control
- *Frame.* In highly structured learning materials, a step that ends by having learners make an active response
- *Active responses.* A response requiring action (e.g., underlining the correct answer)

These concepts allow us to think about questions regarding teaching. For example, should we rely only on positive reinforcement? How small should our instructional steps be? How much modeling should we use in addition to verbal explanations?

Cognitive theories of learning introduce a different set of concepts. For example:

- *Insight.* Seeing all at once the solution to a problem (i.e., "Aha!")
- *Assimilation.* The incorporation of new ideas into an existing cognitive structure
- *Cognitive structure.* An interrelated set of concepts, beliefs, and information that a person has in his or her mind
- *Cognitive dissonance.* Discrepancy, incongruity, or gap between existing knowledge and a new learning task or experience
- *Spiral curriculum.* Successively returning to an idea at increasing levels of sophistication
- *Reception versus discovery learning.* Presentation of content to learners in final form versus allowing the learners to figure it out for themselves
- *Meaningful versus rote learning.* Content being related to the learner's cognitive structure in a nonarbitrary fashion versus the learner's acquiring information that he or she does not integrate into cognitive structure
- *Advance organizers.* Introductory material that acts as a cognitive framework for subsequent instruction
- *Short- versus long-term memory.* One aspect of information storage that is very limited in capacity versus another aspect of information storage that is virtually unlimited in capacity but from which retrieval is often difficult

These concepts allow us to raise further questions about learning: For example, how can we deepen the learners' insights into the meaning of the content we teach? What sorts of advance organizers will help people learn the new material meaningfully? How much cognitive dissonance is productive?

To make matters more complicated, behaviorists and cognitive learning theorists share certain terminology also, although they typically attach different meanings to each term and reach different conclusions. For example, behaviorists claim that errors should be minimized so as to avoid learning them, whereas cognitivists claim that people learn best from their errors.

Behaviorists and cognitive learning theorists also agree on certain general principles, although they may explain them differently. Thus they are both likely to claim that attention, modeling, and practice with feedback are likely to improve performance, but they will explain why in very different theoretical terms.

These basic differences would likely result in different views regarding some common teaching practices. For example:

- *Setting up a laboratory experiment.* Behavioristic approach: The laboratory is for training learners in laboratory skills and scientific behaviors. Cognitive approach: The laboratory gives the learners an opportunity to make a discovery and to confront some evidence that challenges or conflicts with their existing ideas.

- *Designing or selecting instructional material (e.g., workbooks, texts, films).* Behavioristic approach: Instructional material should build complex skills out of simpler prerequisite skills, attempting to minimize learner errors by proceeding in small enough steps. Cognitive approach: Instructional material should present the entire framework at the outset (perhaps by using an analogy or a good example), with the remainder of the material successively adding refinement, sophistication, and detail to the framework while allowing the students to learn from mistakes and to figure out some things for themselves through intelligent guessing.

- *Giving tests.* Behavioristic approach: Tests directly measure the attainment of the teacher's objectives, letting the teacher know whether the class has mastered the objective and giving the learner positive reinforcement, thereby increasing the strength of the behavior. Cognitive approach: Tests offer highly indirect indicators of what is really going on inside a learner's head (e.g., conceptual development), allowing the teacher to analyze student misconceptions and errors and giving the learners information they can use as a basis for modifying ideas and performance. The behaviorist believes that anything with meaning can be observed and measured, whereas the cognitivist believes that many important things we learn are unobservable and therefore cannot be measured in any direct sense.

Consider the following case.

Adrienne's field experience consists of tutoring a ninth-grade boy who is having difficulty with mathematics. Although his class is now studying algebra, the cooperating teacher informs her that Jeff has some gaps in his math preparation. For one thing, he does not seem to know what to do when given a problem requiring the conversion of decimals to fractions and vice versa. Adrienne has found two sets of instructional materials that she can use as a resource for her tutoring session.

One set[22] presents math in programmed form with exercises involving practice drill. Questions are presented in a form that can be answered briefly. For example:

1. Fill in the blanks:
   $3.111 = 3 + 1/10 + 1/100 + 1/1000$ (The first example is a model answer.)
   $7.652 = 7 + 6/ + 5/ + 2/$
   $95.015 = 95 + 0/ + 1/ + 5/$

The second set of materials presents math using drawings and manipulatives in which the learner is expected to make educated guesses, to explain how he or she arrived at a particular answer, and to relate the math content to everyday experiences.

Which materials should Adrienne use with Jeff? What reasons can you give to support your claim? Do you find your preferred approach to this situation to be more behavioristic (the first set of materials) or cognitive (the second set)?
▶

What else do you need to know in order to answer this question? Do you think that your psychological theory depends on the subject matter? What if the subject matter were spelling? What if it were writing?
▶

As expected, behaviorist and cognitive theorists also differ in their explanations of motivation:

> Behavioral psychologists suggest that behavior is determined by past reinforcements and the contingencies in the present environment (i.e., a concern with incentives, habits), . . . and thus more concerned with observable behavior. Cognitive psychologists believe that people decide what they want to achieve, and that their thought processes control behavior. . . . [Therefore, they] are most concerned with perceptions (e.g., discrepancies), information processing, understanding, and curiosity.[23]

Thus, whereas behavioral psychologists talk about *selecting* and *fixing responses* through *reinforcement* and *eliminating* or *extinguishing* others,[24] cognitive psychologists talk about how people perceive and think about themselves and about their success:

> Behaviorists place more emphasis upon external rewards and the deliberate and systematic arrangement of reinforcement contingencies, whereas cognitive theorists place more emphasis upon internal rewards and related cognitive processes.[25]

Behaviorists emphasize extrinsic motivation, and cognitivists stress intrinsic motivation. Many cognitivists believe that curiosity is a natural and spontaneous characteristic of all people, especially children. Other, more eclectic educators believe that curiosity and intrinsic interest are unreliable sources of motivation for the majority of learners and extrinsic rewards must be used initially to involve learners in productive tasks. Once involved, the tasks themselves will often supply intrinsic motivation. What is your view?

▶

Whether your view emphasizes extrinsic or intrinsic rewards, you probably have fairly strong beliefs about competition as a motivator. Perhaps you agree with Johnson and Johnson:

> Competition is threatening and discouraging to those who believe they cannot win and many students will withdraw or only half-try in competitive situations. The whole area of intrinsic motivation shows that motivation does not depend upon competition. Even in extrinsic motivation situations, competition will exist only when there is a limited amount of the reinforcer which cannot be shared with everyone, and when everyone believes he has a chance of winning.[26]

If you agree with Johnson and Johnson, you will likely prefer cooperative classroom environments, not only for motivational purposes but also for the contribution of cooperative environments to social development.

However, you may disagree with them and believe instead that competition is a fact of life and that, regardless of whether it heightens motivation, it is nevertheless an important lesson to be learned in schools in its own right.

Consider your own view of the role of competition and cooperation in the classroom. Think about your own classroom and whether it would emphasize a cooperative or competitive environment. Maybe your answer would vary with different learners.

Consider, for example, some common teaching practices from the perspective of your beliefs about motivation:

- If you were marking student papers, consider whether you would let the entire class know who did the best or whether individual success should be a private matter. Think about the emphasis of your comments on the papers, whether for reinforcement (e.g., praise), for challenging student responses and for raising further questions, or for both purposes.

▶

- If you were organizing the classroom for a set of tasks (e.g., experiments, math problems, art projects, map work), consider whether you would want to organize students into groups or if you would prefer to have them work individually. Would you want students to cooperate on the work or to compete with one another? When choosing the problems or projects on which they work, how important would it be to you that students be initially interested in the work?

▶

Maybe a course in educational psychology has already challenged your beliefs on learning and motivation by presenting alternative views. Maybe such a challenge lies in front of you. Educational psychology has the potential to help you understand the psychological assumptions on which many of your beliefs rest, to help you reconsider those assumptions, and to give you a technical vocabulary to discuss issues of learning and motivation.

Diversity of Learners

TEACHER 1: It's only fair to treat all learners equally.

TEACHER 2: Yes, but we must respond to their individual needs.

STUDENT TEACHER: But which one of you is right?

In a one-on-one teaching situation, we typically respond to a learner as an individual. When we are faced with 30 learners, the complexity of the situation multiplies. How we view learners and how we treat them in group situations is crucial to our teaching. Whether we perceive each learner as unique or as a member of a category (e.g., slow, disabled, poor, disruptive) and whether we treat learners equally regardless of their differences (or differently because of their differences) determine many of our teaching practices. For example, opinions differ about the teacher's allocation of time, based on special learner needs, and the individualization of objectives, content, pace, method of instruction, standards, and rules.

People disagree about special considerations for special learners partly because they disagree about what qualifies as a special need. Both sociology and psychology provide concepts to describe differences among learners; that is, these disciplines provide a variety of labels for categories of "specialness." Although particular schools and agencies have particular policies with regard to special needs, ultimately the teacher decides which of the characteristics are relevant to teaching practices (e.g., what to expect of learners, how much time to give them, what rules they must follow).

Let us begin with a list of general learner characteristics drawn from psychology and sociology: IQ, gender, SES, ethnicity, race, sexual orientation, personality type, developmental stage, family lifestyle, attention span, reading level, and learning differences.

Also consider a list of labels for students drawn from these two disciplines:

gifted and talented
at risk
students with learning disabilities
anxious

highly verbal
only child
hyperactive
oppositional
concrete operational
creative
attention deficit

Also think about another list, not necessarily drawn from psychology and sociology, but nevertheless part of the everyday language of educators:

"jock"
hardworking or lazy
over- or underachiever
college bound or terminal
bright or slow
immature or serious

Of course, none of these lists is exhaustive. But it is important to remember that there are many possible ways to label and categorize learners.

By studying particular schools and communities in depth, some sociologists identify the different ways in which teachers and administrators treat different students, particularly those of differing SES. These researchers note that depending on how they categorize a student, teachers apply different rules, employ different sanctions when rules are broken, have different academic and occupational expectations, apply different academic standards, seek different amounts of student input in instructional decision making, allocate different amounts of instructional time, and teach different content. Such practices may tend to limit students' opportunities for upward social mobility and might act as a set of self-fulfilling prophecies regarding the relationship between SES or race and achievement. That is, students may live up to their teachers' expectations.

However, the point is not to claim that we should ignore all differences among learners, avoid individualization, and not tailor our teaching to the learners' needs. Treating learners as unique individuals is not the same as labeling and then treating them as members of groups. By categorizing learners, we might stereotype and obscure their individuality. More importantly, to some sociologists, labeling and grouping learners runs the risk of limiting the educational opportunity of some students while maximizing it for others. That is, there is always the danger that, despite our good intentions, we may be practicing a subtle form of discrimination. Use the following scenario to think about the effects of labeling and assumptions that go along with defining diversity.

After completing a school-wide survey on student learning traits, you find that many of your students now label themselves as being auditory, visual, or kinesthetic learners. You must decide how best to use your skills as a teacher to reach different types of learners. Do you differentiate instruction, matching each learner style with appropriate instruction (i.e., manipulatives for kinesthetic learners, videos for visual learners)? Or do provide the same instruction for all students and make sure you rotate through the different styles continually? Is it more important to expose learners to various approaches to learning or to focus on using their existing learning styles exclusively? How difficult or easy might it be to accommodate all three learning styles in your teaching?

Do you have different expectations for different groups of students, based on their membership in those groups? Do you plan to group learners in your classroom? If so, on what basis? Would the different groups get different amounts of your time or different materials? What undesirable short- or long-term consequences of this differential treatment should you be careful about?

▶

Regardless of whether you plan to group learners, your class is likely to be a heterogeneous mixture of learners. No matter how homogeneous the learners appear, the learners will certainly differ with regard to personality, interests, family background, and intellectual ability, among other things. As a teacher, your responsibility is typically to respect these and other differences while implementing a common curriculum.

If you teach more than one class, the classes will differ in composition. How do you plan to deal with the diversity of learners? What is your attitude toward learners from backgrounds different from your own? How could you use their diversity as a resource for your teaching? How could you make your lessons more multicultural?

▶

We have just reviewed some sociological reasons for the diversity in learning. Now we can explore examples of the psychological differences in the way people learn. It is safe to say that people learn in many different ways, some in measurably better ways than others. Some youths succeed at memorization, others learn best from their peers, and others need to have hands-on experience in order to best facilitate learning.[27] Dr. Mel Levine, a professor of pediatrics, suggests that we grow into well-adjusted and well-rounded people when eight neurodevelopmental systems are stimulated and exercised regularly. These eight systems include attention control, memory, language, special ordering, sequential ordering, motor, higher thinking, and social thinking. Every child with whom you come in contact has, as Dr. Levine puts it, "a mind's profile, a partly hidden spreadsheet of personal strengths and weaknesses."[28] As this child goes through his or her day, many of these eight neurodevelopmental systems are tested. Because of our profiles some of us are naturally better at some tasks than at others.

Are you better at memorizing lists than you are at sports or vice versa? Maybe you know someone who is very good at doing multistep and complex math problems, but who is also seemingly unable to interact smoothly in social settings? These are just some examples that illustrate the fact that we are all equipped with tools that enable us to interact with ease or with friction in the society in which we live and work. Imagine that you were a student whose mind's profile was not suited to the expectations and/or demands of the school you attended. Do you think it would be difficult to get along there? Students who possess mind profiles that do not match traditional learning models often suffer from feelings of extreme frustration and disappointment. Many students who fail in school do so not because they are unintelligent, but because they are not stimulated by the process of being educated.[29] A mind's profile is formed through a combination of factors, most of which the child realistically has no direct control over. However, if you feel that your mind's profile is not compatible with the world you know and live in, there is still plenty of hope for you, no matter what your age. Dr. Levine is confident that it is "never too late to strengthen your mind."

As a student doing your fieldwork with youths, it is important that you be aware of the existence of a mind's profile, both your own and those of the students with whom you work. As a volunteer placed in a school or in another educational setting, you will have the opportunity to build relationships with youths where you can try to assess your students' profiles. If you can do this, you can then help them to exercise areas of their neurodevelopment that are in need of a workout or by working around them. You can adjust your curriculum to work with a mind's profile by adding hands-on instruction, by removing memorization components, or by encouraging communication skills through structured role-playing.

At first glance, it may seem like an easy fix for a school to vary its educational framework to meet the needs of the individual learner. In practice, it turns out to be a very difficult proposition. It is for this reason that many schools recognize the educational power of extracurricular agencies and benefit of people like you, who are intensely interested in working with youths, but who may have no formal certifications or training in the public school system. These people and organizations often have the flexibility to offer students new ways of learning and new ways of finding and cultivating their own strengths and gifts. If you someday choose to be a classroom teacher, you may never be able to be as flexible with your students as you can be now as a volunteer.

Knowledge

The subject matter is typically taken for granted as the stable "stuff" of teaching, and yet it is the center of a very important set of issues affecting daily teaching practice. Traditionally, debates about knowledge in philosophy of education have concerned the nature of truth. Is a claim about the world true in an absolute sense or only in a relative sense? How is truth determined? Different philosophies propose different views of truth: truth as the coherence of ideas for idealists, truth as correspondence to reality for realists, truth as the product of reason and intuition of neo-Thomists, truth as what works for experimentalists, or truth as existential choice for existentialists.[30]

How do you view knowledge in your subject matter? Do you think of learning your subject matter as absorbing ideas (idealism), mastering facts and information (realism), training the intellect (neo-Thomism), problem solving (experimentalism), or finding the self (existentialism)?[31]

▶

More recently, philosophical debates about knowledge have concerned the way in which scientific ideas change and science progresses. Today's philosophers of science, such as Thomas Kuhn and Stephen Toulmin, reject the nineteenth-century "empiricist" view that science changes as a result of the accumulation of new facts and observations and the refinement of generalizations based on them. They also reject the empiricist requirement that scientists observe what is "really there" and be objective in their descriptions. In contrast, modern philosophy of science contends that science changes as a result of the failure of current theory to solve important scientific problems. Old theories are rejected and replaced by new ones based on assumptions significantly different from those of the theories they are replacing. This "conceptual change" view argues further that our concepts and theories determine what we see. People with different theories can live in different perceptual worlds. Thus, what scientists see is affected by their scientific theories and concepts.[32]

These philosophical views have important implications for teaching practice. Consider, for example, three contrasting views on teaching as they relate to empiricist and conceptual change philosophies of science.[33]

A *didactic* view of teaching, primarily aimed at transmitting knowledge, relies on clear explanations, experiments, or demonstrations employed in support of the explanations, and guides discussions by using convergent questions, hints, and explanations. This view assumes learning to be the addition of new knowledge—a view consistent with empiricist ideas about the growth of knowledge.

A *discovery* view of teaching assumes that "students develop knowledge for themselves through active investigation and discovery."[34] The teacher focuses on student observations and measurements, acceptance of student responses to questions, and an absence of teacher presentations. This view is also fundamentally empiricist, particularly in its emphasis on objective observations "uncontaminated" by theories and in its claim that knowledge develops inductively from observations.

Both of these views have been criticized by the *interactionist* view,[35] a view based on a conceptual change philosophy. The *interactionist* view of teaching argues that students arrive in the classroom with well-formed, though often incorrect, ideas. Didactic teaching rejects or ignores these ideas. Discovery teaching allows students to develop further and refine their naive ideas through active experimentation, regardless of whether their naive ideas are true. In contrast with these two views, the interactionist view is more adversarial, recognizing the necessary interaction among students' naive ideas, their empirical observation, and the curriculum content. Such a view requires the teacher

> to bring out the students' preconceptions, provide a base of relevant experience and observations, challenge the students' misconceptions with appropriate questions and evidence, clearly present the . . . conception (to be learned), and help the student to realize the greater power and usefulness of the new conception.[36]

Although these contrasting views refer primarily to science teaching, how well do you think they relate to other subject areas? To what extent will your students come with preconceptions that will conflict with what you plan to teach?
▶

Obviously, discussions of knowledge are not independent of discussions of learning. After all, "to come to know" and "to learn" are two different ways of expressing similar ideas. The distinction between the psychological term *learn* and the philosophical term *know* rests primarily on the kinds of questions the two disciplines ask regarding knowledge and its acquisition. Whereas educational psychologists investigate the actual processes through which people acquire knowledge, philosophers explore the nature, limits, and validity of knowledge, rationality, and inquiry. Therefore, it should not be surprising to find psychological theories that complement philosophical views on knowledge. Simply (or simplistically) stated, behaviorism is a modern expression of traditional empiricism, and cognitive psychology (particularly the work of Piaget, Kohlberg, and modern information-processing theorists such as Donald Norman) is consistent with a "conceptual change" viewpoint.

Think through the following scenario to see how you view the role of knowledge production in the classroom.

Your principal has just finished watching you teach a math lesson and tells you that things went well but offers you a word of advice: "You know, every time you teach students something, you rob them of the opportunity to discover it. Why don't you give the students a problem and let them work it out for themselves? It will take a while, but in the end it will be much more satisfying" Would you be willing to try this approach? How long would you let the students work on the answer? What would you be sacrificing from your point of view by trying this method? When has your own education been most exciting—while you were discovering and learning or when you came to know the answer?

Not only do philosophical orientations relate to psychological theories, they also have sociological dimensions. We have already seen that knowledge to the sociologists may be considered a means of control. Berlak and Berlak point out additional sociological dimensions of knowledge. They suggest that the traditional philosophical distinction between knowledge viewed as "given" (e.g., in realism) versus knowledge viewed as "problematic" (e.g., in experimentalism) has significant sociological implications:

> Patterns that are predominantly *given* would, we suppose, convey unquestioning reverence and respect for the public knowledge transmitted by society through its agents, and ultimately for the society and its institutions as well, while heavily *problematic* patterns would convey a disposition towards criticism and analysis, of culture and society, and encourage creativity.[37]

Further, they suggest that teachers may view knowledge differently for different types of learners (see the issue of "diversity") and for different subjects. If knowledge as given (e.g., emphasizing facts) underlies our teaching of one racial, ethnic, or SES group but not others (e.g., emphasizing critical thinking), we may be implying that certain types of people should learn to criticize their culture and society and to be creative, but other types of people should learn to accept and adjust to society's institutions. Berlak and Berlak also point out that knowledge in some realms (e.g., mathematics and history) is treated as given and certain, and knowledge in other realms (e.g., literature) is treated as problematic.[38]

In your view, is the knowledge in some subject matters more certain than in others? Should some kinds of students come to view your subject matter as certain while others develop a view of it as being less certain, more problematic? How do the tests and homework that teachers give and the way in which teachers administer and mark them convey a teacher's position on this issue?

▶

Role of the Teacher

"Be a real person." *(Carl Rogers)*

"Children don't want teachers to be their friends, they want someone to look up to." *(Common advice to new teachers)*

Many sociologists point out that schools are both agencies of socialization and bureaucratic organizations. In their attempts at socialization, they try to promote the kinds of learning and development they deem necessary for the growth of children into responsible, productive, and competent adults. For many educators, this process requires warm interpersonal relationships tailored to the uniqueness of each individual. However, as bureaucratic agencies, schools often provide impersonal and uniform treatment. Thus, sociologically speaking, there is a conflict of roles.

Will you as a teacher be formal and businesslike with your class, maintaining sufficient social distance from the learners, or will you try to be more informal and friendly? How much of a shift in roles must occur when you move from one side of the teacher's desk to the other?

▶

If you ask "experts" for their advice on these questions, you are likely to hear conflicting views. The answers seem to depend a great deal on whom you ask. For example, compare the sociologist Willard Waller with Carl Rogers. According to Waller:

> Social distance is characteristic of the personal entanglements of teachers and students. It is a necessity where the subordination of one person to another is required, for distance makes possible that recession of feeling without which the authority of another is not tolerable. . . . Between adult and child is an irreducible social distance that seems at times an impassable gulf. The distance arises from the fact that the adult has absorbed the heritage of the group, and represents therefore in some sense the man plus the wisdom of all his ancestors, whereas the child is much more the natural and uncultivated man, and from the fact that the adult has found his place in the world and the child has not. . . . To the natural distance between adult and child is added a greater distance when the adult is a teacher and the child is a student, and this distance arises mainly from the fact that the teacher must give orders to the child; they cannot know each other, for we can never know a person at whom we only peer through institutional bars. Formality arises in the teacher-pupil relationship as a means of maintaining social distance, which in turn is a means to discipline. . . . Most important of the means whereby distance is maintained . . . is that classroom procedure which defers the situation in an impersonal manner and excludes possibilities of spontaneous human interaction. This is the dry, matter-of-fact, formal procedure of the classroom, which gives nothing and asks nothing of personality, but is always directed at the highly intellectualized matter to be studied.[39]

Consider the validity of this statement as a description of the reality of classroom teaching. Maybe you can infer Waller's attitude toward formal teaching: a necessary evil, a necessary good, or neutral. It might be interesting to consider how he would respond to this excerpt from Rogers:

> What are these qualities, these attitudes, that facilitate learning? . . . Perhaps the most basic of these essential attitudes is realness or genuineness. When the facilitator is a real person, being what she is, entering into a relationship with the learner without presenting a front or a facade, she is much more likely to be effective. This means that the feelings that she is experiencing are available to her, available to her awareness, that she is able to live these feelings, be them, and able to communicate them if appropriate. It means that she comes into a direct personal encounter with the learner, meeting her on a person-to-person basis. It means that she is *being* herself, not denying herself. . . . Thus, she is a person to her students, not a faceless embodiment of a curricular requirement nor a sterile tube through which knowledge is passed from one generation to the next. . . . It is obvious that this attitudinal set, found to be effective in psychotherapy, is sharply in contrast with the tendency of most teachers to show themselves to their pupils simply as roles. It is quite customary for teachers rather consciously to put on the mask, the role, the facade of being a teacher and to wear this facade all day removing it only when they have left the school at night.[40]

Rogers's view is consistent with many "open education" writers around 1970 in the United States, such as Charles Silberman:

> Informal education relieves the teacher of the terrible burden of omniscience. . . . To the formal teacher, admitting ignorance means loss of dignity. . . . In an informal classroom, by contrast, the teacher is the facilitator [note the term *facilitator* in both Rogers's and Silberman's writing] rather than the source of learning, the source being the child himself. . . . The consequence is an atmosphere in which everyone is learning together. . . . Most important, however, the free day classroom relieves the teacher of the necessity of being a timekeeper, traffic cop, and disciplinarian. In a formal classroom, a large proportion of the teacher's time and an extraordinary amount of energy

are consumed simply by the need to maintain order and control. ("I cannot begin until all talking is stopped and every eye is on me!") In the informal classroom, the discipline problem withers away, in part because children are not required to sit still and be silent. . . . A[n] [informal] teacher with forty years' experience remarks, "I try to be informal. I mean, I try to make this situation as much as possible like a family group sitting around a fireplace or around a table when some question has come up and they're discussing it."[41]

Consider your own view of the Rogers/Silberman position. Are they being realistic? Perhaps the conflict between Waller's sociological and Rogers's psychotherapeutic analysis stems from a difference between a description of the ways things are and a proposal for the way things ought to be. Maybe different disciplines of knowledge (here, sociology and psychotherapy) offer different, even conflicting, perspectives on classroom teaching.
▶

More importantly, what is your view regarding the informal/formal issue? How informal or formal do you plan to be, and how do you plan to express your preferred role? Think about your role in terms of the sorts of clothing you plan to wear, how you will expect your students to address you, the rules for determining speaking order in the classroom (e.g., hand raising), where and how you will position yourself in the classroom, how strict you will be, what you will do when one of your students tries to approach you on a personal matter (either yours or the student's), and what sort of differences there are between your in-class and out-of-class voice. Waller points out that these aspects of a teacher's behavior all affect the teacher's prestige.

Review the following scenario and compare your thoughts with those of others.

It is your first day of teaching, and you have heard that your class is "very rowdy," "a bunch of angels," and "a mixed bag." You do not know which of these descriptions is accurate. You need to decide what you will say to this group of students on your first meeting. Because you do not know which group you really have, what will you say? Why? Can you easily take on a role that works well with any group? What would that role be? Is it easier (for you/for students) to start off the year being informal or formal? Why?
▶

School and Society

"Teaching is subversive activity." *(Neil Postman and Charles Weingartner)*

"Dare the school build a new social order?" *(George S. Counts)*

"Schools merely reproduce the social order and perpetuate its class stratifications." *(various neo-Marxists)*

"Don't make waves!" *(Anonymous)*

Perhaps one or more of these quotations reflects your view of teaching.

Of course, schools are for learning. They are a society's primary means for transmitting the cultural heritage from one generation to the next. But some sociologists notice "two other fundamental and inseparable purposes: (1) they keep lower-class students from competing equally with middle-class students, and (2) they serve to legitimate the political and social system."[42] Some sociologists view schooling as a "competitive struggle for social and economic rewards. It is essentially a tug-of-war between the middle and lower classes, with the upper classes literally above the battle."[43]

But what roles do teachers play in this process? Although our personal political posture does not necessarily influence our daily teaching practices, most of us nevertheless have rather deep political convictions. These convictions may affect the teaching of social studies more than the teaching of math, but it is difficult to escape the effect altogether in any teaching situation. "Either a teaching activity serves to integrate children in the current social order, or it provides children with the knowledge, attitudes or skills to deal critically and creatively with that reality in order to improve it."[44] The contexts of our teaching can never be ignored for long.

The teacher is the primary political socializing agent for the child, so the teacher's political posture is crucial.

> The teacher represents *the* authoritative spokesman of society, for the teacher is usually the first model of political authority the beginning student encounters.[45]

With teachers playing such a crucial role in the socialization of learners, some sociologists see the political orientation of teachers as a key factor affecting the process of education:

> The conservatism apparent in teachers is best understood, perhaps, by considering them as advocates of the interests of the middle class. Teachers prefer to do regular rather than radical things, and they do not encourage their students to participate in politics other than in the most accepted and established fashions. This interpretation is based upon the assumption that teachers charged with the responsibilities of injecting system maintenance values into the educational subculture encourage their students to become good citizens, and in so doing, do not offer students an alternative to acceptance of the *status quo*.[46]

These sociological claims regarding the purposes of schooling and the socialization of students and teachers may strike you as obvious or as absurd. Even if you accept these claims as valid, you may either applaud or deplore schools and teachers that serve these functions.

How do you see yourself in relation to the school and society? How politically conservative are you? How comfortable are you with people of more radical political persuasion? To what extent do you believe that the school is the *cause* of social inequalities? How supportive of "middle-class" values are you? For example, to what extent do you agree with each of the following middle-class beliefs:

- A person's career is the most important determinant of status in our society.
- My children should have the same educational opportunities I have had.
- A "good" school is one that is academically oriented.
- Education is the pathway to economic achievement.

▶

Another way to assess your own political posture as a teacher is to consider classroom problems: Are the problems you face as a teacher basically educational problems solvable through educational means? Or do most of the problems require structural changes in schools and society? Clearly, an affirmative answer to this last question reflects a less conservative view. Although the terms *conservative* and *progressive* have acquired many new and misleading connotations, they still denote two ends of a continuum that describes these basic issues.

From a philosophical point of view, this issue could be treated as a debate between reconstructionists and conservatives, between philosophers such as Theodore Brameld and William Bagley:

> [Brameld] While repudiating nothing of the constructive achievements of other educational theories, reconstructionism commits itself, first of all, to the renascence of modern culture. It is infused with a profound conviction that we are in the midst of a revolutionary period out of which should emerge nothing less than the control of the industrial system, of public services, and of cultural and natural resources by and for the common people who, throughout the ages, have struggled for a life of security, decency, and peace for themselves and their children.[47]

> [Bagley] The very time to avoid chaos in the schools is when something akin to chaos characterizes the social environment. . . . The very time to emphasize in the schools the values that are relatively certain and stable is when the social environment is full of uncertainty and when standards are crumbling. Education follows, it does not lead. If education is to be a stabilizing force it means that the school must discharge what is in effect a disciplinary function. The materials of instruction, the methods of teaching, and the life of the school as a social organization must exemplify *and idealize* consideration, cooperation, cheerfulness, fidelity to duty and to trust, courage and perseverance in the face of disappointment, aggressive effort toward doing the task that one's hand finds to do and doing it as well as one can, loyalty to friend and family and those for whom one is responsible, a sense of fact and a willingness to face facts, clear and honest thinking. These may not be eternal values, but one may venture a fairly confident prediction that they will be just as significant a thousand years from now as they have ever been in the past.[48]

You might examine whether we are "in the midst of a revolutionary period," how "stable" our values are, and whether education follows or leads the society. What is your position regarding the reconstructionist–conservative debate, and how would your position affect your conduct as a teacher?

Write your response to the following scenario.

At a faculty meeting, you and the other teachers are informed that you can now begin to use your position to help your high school students better understand the cultural, political, and social forces acting on them. As an example, the principal states that you can "tell Kelly that she should resist her father's push for her to join the armed forces and consider the Peace Corps instead." How would you react? Do you feel uncomfortable talking about social and political issues in school? Would you rather keep school focused on academics and leave politics outside the front door?

▶

Interrelations among the Six Issues

As with most other things in education, these six issues are highly interrelated. Beliefs about learning and motivation relate directly to beliefs about knowledge, the teacher's role, and control. For example, a person with a belief in cooperative learning environments (*learning*) might be likely to value a close relationship with pupils (*teacher role*), to base context decisions on the children's interests (*knowledge* and *motivation*), and to let the children participate fully in setting rules for classroom operations (*control*).

Such a teacher might be labeled "informal." In contrast with this teacher is one who emphasizes grades (extrinsic *motivation*) and, perhaps, competition (*learning*), teaches mostly facts without worrying too much about how they relate to children's past experience (*knowledge*), sets rules of conduct, and enforces them strictly but fairly (*control*) in a businesslike manner (*teacher role*). This teacher might be labeled "formal."

Labels such as formal/informal, traditional/progressive, and authoritarian/ democratic might work well for extremes in teacher perspectives, but the vast majority of teachers' perspectives are too complex for such oversimplifications. Although our beliefs on one issue relate to our beliefs on another, the relationship is not entirely predictable. For example, a teacher who tries to develop a "good group" might have a self-image of a strong group leader, even as a benevolent dictator.[49] This emphasis on the group can lead to the teacher's exerting strong control of classroom behavior, being particularly strict with "uncooperative" behaviors.

Each of the six issues is far too general for use to resolve in any definitive manner. The questions used to present them can be answered similarly: "It all depends!" Actually it all depends on the four common features we discussed earlier. It all depends on who the *teacher* is; who the *learners* are; what the *subject matter* is; and in what grade level, type of school, and community (i.e., *context*) the teaching is situated. Let us examine an example of the way the resolution of basic issues depends on what the subject matter is, who the learners are, what the context is, and who the teacher is.

Mrs. Borden has definite views about *subject matter*, but her views differ for each subject.[50] She monitors the morning's work in the three Rs much more closely than she does the afternoon activities—arts and crafts, music, and dramatic play. For the three Rs, she keeps careful records of both time spent and accomplishments. She treats the arts, creative play, and social development more as rewards for work in the basics than as significant subjects in their own right. Social studies and science are learned through project work in which the pupils are allowed to choose their topics.

When we look at the differential treatment of *learners* in addition to subject matter, Mrs. Borden's resolution of the issues becomes striking, particularly with regard to the consequences of her practices for her pupils. Her "slower" pupils are those who cannot quickly memorize written words and/or have not acquired decoding skills. These pupils receive more step-by-step, less broad, more extrinsically motivated, less personally relevant instruction. For example, they spend more time memorizing words out of context and more time reading from books that control vocabulary in terms of structurally similar words (e.g., *hat, cat, mat,* etc.). Perhaps because these stories lack any interest value (and, therefore, intrinsic motivation), these "slower" children are constantly pushed to "get on with it." Because some of these children come from backgrounds somewhat different from those of the other children, the content of all the instruction is less likely to relate to the life they experience after school hours and beyond the school's walls.

As the *context* of the teaching shifts, so too will the teacher's resolution of the issues. As these "slower" children move up in grade level, they may spend more time being "remediated," receiving more extrinsic motivation and less meaningful and interesting content from their remedial reading *teacher*, who may increasingly treat them as clients, leaving them dependent on their teachers for help. Meanwhile, their "regular" teachers are likely to exert far greater control over their "faster" classmates. Many aspects of this differential treatment could be accentuated if these pupils are from low-SES neighborhoods and if the teacher is middle class and unfamiliar with low-SES people.

Notice the terrain we have traveled in this chapter. Our discussion of *control* centered on a sociological analysis of rules, socialization, and the curriculum. However, at the end of this section we mentioned psychological and philosophical dimensions of control. We discussed behavioral and cognitive psychological dimensions of *learning* and *motivation.* We viewed the *diversity of learners* from a predominantly sociological perspective, on labeling and grouping people, though the labels themselves derive from both sociology and psychology. Whether knowledge is certain or problematic was the focus of our philosophical treatment of the *knowledge* issue, though we also analyzed knowledge as a sociological issue. When we discussed the *role of the teacher,* we compared one sociological view of social distance with one psychological view of genuineness. Our discussion of *school* and *society* included the socialization of teachers and students and a comparison between two philosophies, reconstructionism and conservatism.

Obviously, each of the six issues serves as a focal point for a divergent set of foundational perspectives. The foundations of education help us raise questions and supply concepts for thinking about our own teaching practices. But the foundations cannot answer these questions. Answers reflect our own personal perspective on teaching, which in turn depend on the situation in which we teach. In order to answer these questions, we must make a commitment to a view on what good teaching is and on what a good teacher does in a particular situation.

NOTES

1. Because of limited space, this book discusses only three of the disciplines: philosophy, psychology, and sociology.
2. These six issues are derived from the work of Ann Berlak and Harold Berlak, *Dilemmas of Schooling* (New York: Methuen, 1981).
3. Willard Waller, *The Sociology of Teaching* (New York: Wiley, 1932).
4. Robert Arnove, "On Sociological Perspective and Educational Problems," in *Education and American Culture,* eds. Elizabeth Steiner, Robert Arnove, and B. Edward McClellan (New York: Macmillan, 1980), p. 6.
5. Emile Durkheim, *Education and Sociology,* trans. Sherwood Fox (Glencoe, IL: The Free Press, 1956).
6. Talcott Parsons, "The School Class as a Social System," *Harvard Educational Review* 29 (Fall 1959), 297–318.
7. Samuel Bowles and Herbert Gintis, *Schooling in Capitalist America: Educational Reform and the Contradictions of Economic Life* (New York: Basic Books, 1976).
8. Waller, *Sociology of Teaching.*
9. Parsons, "The School Class."
10. Philip Jackson, *Life in Classrooms* (New York: Holt, Rinehart and Winston, 1968).
11. I borrowed this last point from Jane Martin, "What Should We Do with a Hidden Curriculum When We Find One?" in *The Hidden Curriculum and Moral Education,* eds. Henry Giroux and David Purpel (Berkeley, CA: McCutchan, 1983).
12. Jean Anyon, "Social Class and the Hidden Curriculum of Work," in *Curriculum and Instruction,* eds. Henry Giroux, Anthony Penna, and William Pinar (Berkeley, CA: McCutchan, 1981).
13. Ronald Corwin, *Militant Professionalism: A Study of Organizational Conflict in High Schools* (New York: Appleton, 1970), p. 234.
14. Basil Bernstein, "On the Classification and Framing of Educational Knowledge," in *Knowledge and Control: New Directions for the Sociology of Knowledge,* ed. Michael Young (London: Collier-Macmillan, 1971).
15. Max Weber, *Essays in Sociology,* trans. and eds. H. Gerth and C. W. Mills (London: Routledge and Kegan Paul, 1952).
16. A. Gramsci, *The Modern Prince and Other Writings* (translation) (New York: Monthly Review Press, 1957).
17. Michael Young, ed., *Knowledge and Control: New Directions for the Sociology of Education* (London: Collier-Macmillan, 1971), p. 36.
18. Ibid.
19. Ibid., p. 38.
20. See, for example, Kenneth Strike, *Liberty and Learning* (Oxford, England: Martin Robertson, 1982).

21. Much of this section is adapted from Thomas Good and Jere Brophy, *Educational Psychology: A Realistic Approach*, 2nd ed. (New York: Holt, Rinehart and Winston, 1980).

22. Cited by S. H. Erlwanger, "Benny's Conception of Rules and Answers in IPI Mathematics," *Journal of Children's Mathematical Behavior*, 1(2) (Autumn 1973), 71–90.

23. Good and Brophy, *Educational Psychology*, pp. 210–211.

24. Ibid.

25. Ibid., p. 212.

26. David Johnson and Roger Johnson, "Instructional Goal Structure: Cooperative, Competitive or Individualistic," *Review of Educational Research*, 44(2) (1974), 218.

27. Howard Gardner, *The Disciplined Mind* (New York: Simon & Schuster, 1999).

28. Mel Levine, *A Mind at a Time* (New York: Simon & Schuster, 2002), p. 35.

29. John Holt, *How Children Fail* (Reading, MA: Merloyd Lawrence, 1995).

30. Van Cleve Morris, *Philosophy and the American School* (Boston: Houghton Mifflin, 1961).

31. Ibid.

32. See Kenneth Strike and George Posner, "Epistemological Perspectives on Conceptions of Curriculum Organization and Learning," in *Review of Research in Education*, ed. Lee Shulman, Vol. 4 (Itasca, IL: F. E. Peacock, 1976); Harold Brown, *Perception, Theory and Commitment: The New Philosophy of Science* (Chicago: University of Chicago Press, 1977).

33. This discussion is based on Edward Smith and Charles Anderson, "The Effects of Teacher's Guides on Teacher Planning and Classroom Instruction in Activity-Based Science." Paper presented at the annual meeting of the American Educational Research Association, Montreal, April 1983.

34. Ibid., p. 19.

35. Smith and Anderson (ibid.) refer to this view as the "conceptual change" view.

36. Ibid., p. 19.

37. Ann Berlak and Harold Berlak, *Dilemmas of Schooling: Teaching and Social Change* (New York: Methuen, 1981), p. 148.

38. Ibid.

39. Waller, *Sociology of Teaching*, pp. 279–280.

40. Carl Rogers, *Freedom to Learn for the 80's* (Columbus, OH: Charles E. Merrill, 1983), pp. 121–122.

41. Charles Silberman, *Crisis in the Classroom: The Remaking of American Education* (New York: Random House, 1970), pp. 267–271.

42. Joseph Scimecca, *Education and Society* (New York: Holt, Rinehart and Winston, 1980), p. 24.

43. Ibid., p. 24.

44. Carl Grant and Kenneth Zeichner, "On Becoming a Reflective Teacher," in *Preparing for Reflective Teaching*, ed. Carl A. Grant (Boston: Allyn & Bacon, 1984), p. 15.

45. Scimecca, *Education and Society*, p. 105.

46. Harmon Zeigler, *The Political Life of American Teachers* (Englewood Cliffs, NJ: Prentice Hall, 1967), pp. 21–22.

47. Theodore Brameld, adapted from *Education for the Emerging Age* (New York: Harper & Row, 1969), pp. 26–27.

48. William Bagley, *Education and Emergent Man* (New York: Ronald Press, 1934), pp. 154–156.

49. See Valerie Janesick, "An Ethnographic Study of a Teacher's Classroom Perspective," unpublished doctoral dissertation, Michigan State University, 1977. See also John Rosemond, *Teen-Proofing* (Kansas City, MO: Andrews & McMeel, 1998) for a discussion of the "benevolent dictator."

50. A fictitious teacher inspired by several teachers described in Berlak and Berlak, *Dilemmas*.

CHAPTER 6

Contributions of Methods Courses

In Chapter 5, we examined the contributions of your foundational studies to your own perspective on teaching; we now turn to the ideas you have learned or will learn in your study of teaching methods. The study of teaching methods is quite diverse. Few generalizations can be made about what people study in methods courses. For the purpose of using these studies as a focus for reflection on teaching, we will examine three aspects of teaching methods: lesson planning, instructional activities, and curriculum emphasis.

Lesson Planning

The first issue to address regarding planning your methods of teaching is the extent to which planning is either necessary or appropriate at this point. Let's assume that your field experience consists of tutoring a sixth-grader who is having trouble with social studies. Obviously, before the first meeting, any lesson planning would be pointless. However, even after meeting the student and discussing the kinds of help she needs, it still may be inappropriate to plan. If your weekly meeting is to help her with her homework, to go over her weekly quiz, and to answer any questions she may have, planning may still be inappropriate. It all depends on the role you are being asked to play.

Suppose, on the other hand, that this sixth-grader is getting poor grades, that you and she decide she needs help preparing for the weekly quiz, and that your weekly session will be used for that purpose. In this case, it is your responsibility to plan the session for this purpose, even if your plans occasionally are set aside in order to deal with problems she brings to the session.

This section of the chapter is about planning lessons. If you find in your field placement that you cannot anticipate what the learners will need, then you might not want to invest much time in planning. In any case, you might still find the material in this chapter useful, because at some point in your field experience, you will likely need to plan a lesson.

Planning Frames

Take the time now to jot down some preliminary plans for your first (or next) session in the field. Start wherever it feels comfortable. Don't worry about the form your plan takes or about the "correctness" of it.[1]

▶

Now let us reflect on the preliminary plan. When teachers begin to plan a lesson, they typically begin with a search for an answer to one or more questions:

1. What do I want the learners to learn?
2. What should I have the learners do?
3. How much time do I need to plan for?
4. What materials will I need?
5. What content should I cover?
6. What will they do and what will I do?
7. What products, responses, reactions, and results do I want to be the outcome of the lesson?
8. What do the learners already know and what kinds of experiences have they already had?

In other words, planning typically begins with a particular concern that focuses the teacher's attention on some aspect of planning:

- Objectives
- Activities
- Time
- Materials
- Content
- Procedures
- Outcomes
- Prior knowledge and experience

Each of these elements can be considered a mental structure, termed a *frame*, that constitutes a functional unit guiding the teacher's thinking. In this case, the thinking consists of planning a lesson, and the frame is thus called a *planning frame*.[2] Although methods courses typically teach that planning should begin with one item from this list (most likely, objectives), in reality, teachers begin with different planning frames, although they eventually give some consideration to all of the questions listed previously. Elementary teachers are more likely to begin with an activities frame, whereas high school teachers are more likely to begin with a content frame. Middle school teachers might begin with either of these two frames.

Before we get locked into an overly simplistic interpretation of teacher planning, we should mention some other factors affecting the choice of planning frame. Subject matter also affects the frame a teacher utilizes in planning. Some subject matter is more loaded with facts (e.g., history), lending itself to a content frame, whereas other subject matter is more experiential (e.g., physical education), lending itself to activity, procedure, and materials frames. Other factors related to the particular situation also affect the choice of an initial planning frame. Teaching a group of children with special interests (e.g., music) or needs (e.g., non-English speaking) might lead to a planning frame that focuses on their special interests or one focusing on their needs, respectively. Planning for a tightly organized lesson to be given within a precise period of time (e.g., a 43-minute period) might lead to planning that begins by asking the question "How should I break up this time period so that my lesson has a well-defined introduction, main body, and conclusion?" (a time frame). The variations are endless.

As suggested in the previous examples of various initial planning frames, the planning frame chosen as the starting point is indicative of a particular *perception* of a situation; a planning frame does not imply an inherent property of a school, classroom, or school subject. It is possible to conceive of high schools that are not more content centered than elementary schools; in fact, there are both notable historical and contemporary examples of problem-centered, interdisciplinary high schools.[3] History is not inherently more factual than other subjects. What we typically conceive of as history taught in schools, however, seems to be quite factual. What we conceive of as a special interest or need that should be addressed, others might not. What I perceive as 43 minutes that need to be allocated, someone else might perceive as an undefined period of time during which some interesting activities can be launched but not completed. Therefore, choice of an initial planning frame may suggest how a teacher perceives a situation and, thus, provide an opportunity to reflect on that teacher's assumptions about teaching.

A recent development in planning and designing curriculum is "backward design." The fundamental questions that are asked when using this model are:

- What are the learning goals?
- What would count as evidence of meeting those goals?
- What are the implied performances that constitute assessment?

Wiggins and McTighe have developed the model and identify its three stages:[4]

1. *Identify desired results.* What should students know and be able to do? What content is worth knowing?
2. *Determine acceptable evidence.* How do we know if students have achieved the goals we established? What counts as evidence?
3. *Plan learning experiences and instruction.* What knowledge, activities, and skills do students need to accomplish the goals?

Proponents of this method state that sophisticated understanding occurs as a result of implementing the design through lesson and unit plans.

Preliminary Plans

Examine your preliminary plans. What was your initial planning frame? That is, which of the eight questions listed earlier were you attempting to answer?
▶

What assumptions underlie this choice of a starting point in planning? More specifically, does the choice of a particular planning frame suggest any assumptions about schools, the subject matter, the learners, or your role as the teacher? Write down your thoughts on this matter.
▶

Instructional Activities

Eventually, planning for teaching requires the choice of some set of activities. These activities range from those that are highly teacher centered, such as lectures and demonstrations, to those that are highly learner centered, such as individual project work and cooperative learning groups.

EXERCISE 6.1

Assessment of Activities

Courses on teaching methods provide students with a variety of activities that a teacher can use. Regardless of whether you have already taken such a course, now is the time to take stock of what you know about these activities by comparing them on the basis of their strengths, weaknesses, and for whom and what they are appropriate. In addition to making an attempt at an objective assessment of activities (though no assessment is ever really objective), add a blatantly subjective element to this assessment. Indicate the extent to which each relevant activity is appropriate for your own personality and style as a teacher. If any of these activities are unfamiliar to you, you might want to look them up in a general methods text.

Activity	Strengths	Weaknesses	Learners	Goals	Appropriateness to my personality
Lecture/demo					
Discussion					
Worksheets					
Cooperative learning					
Individual projects					
Group projects					
Role playing					
Simulations/ games					
Debates					
Field trips					
Laboratories					
Films/tapes/ slides					
Other					

Curriculum Emphasis[5]

Every time we teach a subject, we give it a particular emphasis. For example, if we teach science, we might find our lessons aimed at one or more of the following emphases:

- Students must learn how to apply scientific principles to our technological and natural environment. (Coping with problems)

- Students must engage in real scientific inquiry themselves, during which time, they examine the interplay between theory and evidence, the adequacy of particular models used to explain physical phenomena, and the tentativeness of scientific knowledge. (Structure of science)
- Science is viewed as a set of skills to be learned rather than as knowledge to be acquired—that is, process rather than product oriented. (Scientific skill development)
- Teachers provide clear explanations, and students accept these ideas. (Transmission of cultural heritage)
- Students demonstrate mastery of content. (Provision of solid foundation)
- Science education examines the growth and change in scientific ideas as a function of human purposes and historical settings. (Science as a cultural institution)

After each emphasis listed, I have summarized the justification (in parentheses) a teacher might propose for teaching science. As you can see, a particular emphasis is based on a particular justification for teaching that subject matter. It should be clear that none of these emphases is correct or incorrect. Each might be "right" in a particular situation—that is, with particular learners—in a particular setting and with a particular teacher.

In addition, your personal history (see Chapter 4) has contributed greatly to the particular emphases you are likely to give to the various subject matters you will teach. If you are preparing to teach a particular subject matter (e.g., English), these two factors probably even contributed to your decision to teach this subject matter in the first place.

EXERCISE 6.2

Justifying Subject Matter

In your fieldwork, you may be responsible for teaching particular subject matters or topics. If this is the case, choose one for which you have been given the greatest degree of autonomy. For this subject matter or topic, try to generate a set of (three to five) possible answers to the following question:

▶   Why study this subject matter or topic? Do not worry if your answers overlap slightly.

▶   Now, for each justification, try to describe a particular emphasis that is consistent with the justification.

▶   Finally, write a statement describing the justification and emphasis that you believe underlies your teaching at your particular field placement.

Theory and Practice

Most methods courses present more than the nuts and bolts of teaching. They also represent a particular set of beliefs about teaching. In your methods courses, you might have focused on the teaching practices. Here, we focus on the underlying beliefs.

For example, on the surface, Reading Recovery is a program designed for students in early primary school who are at risk of educational failure. It attempts to teach a set of reading strategies based on what the child already knows using a basic lesson format. At the same time, Reading Recovery is also a set of beliefs about learning. These beliefs include the following: (1) Each child is an active learner; (2) children bring their own meaning to the books they read; (3) good readers use particular strategies that weak readers can learn; and (4) children learn to use multiple sources of information when they read or write. Notice that all these beliefs focus on the basic issue of learning.

Other topics in methods courses might focus on other issues. The six issues presented in Chapter 5 can function as a useful road map for charting the beliefs of each topic presented in your methods courses. You should be able to relate each topic to one or more of these basic issues. For example, multicultural education focuses on issues related to both diversity and the relation between school and society, whereas assertive discipline focuses on issues of control and the role of the teacher. By way of contrast, constructivist methods of teaching mathematics and science focus on issues related to both knowledge and learning.

EXERCISE 6.3

Identifying Issues

Take stock of the topics presented in your methods courses. For as many as possible, identify which of the six issues presented in Chapter 5 relate most directly to the beliefs underlying the topic. Then, specifically identify as many of the underlying beliefs as you can for each of these topics.

Here is a list of possible topics. Some items were not included in your particular methods courses. And, no doubt, there were topics you encountered that are not on this list. Use the list only as a starting point for this exercise.

Whole language
Constructivism
Multicultural education
Process writing
Cooperative learning
Discovery learning
Individualized instruction
Reading Recovery
Behavioral objectives
Portfolio assessment
Other topics

NOTES

1. Edward L. Smith and Neil B. Sendelbach, "The Programme, the Plans and the Activities of the Classroom: The Demands of Activity-Based Science," in *Innovation in the Science Curriculum*, ed. John Olson (London: Croon Helm, 1982).
2. Ibid., pp. 101–105.
3. See Lawrence A. Cremin, *The Transformation of the School* (New York: Knopf, 1961), for historical examples.
4. Grant Wiggins and Jay McTighe, *Understanding by Design* (New Jersey: Prentice Hall, 2005).
5. Adapted from Douglas Roberts, "Developing the Concept of 'Curriculum Emphasis' in Science Education," *Science Education*, 60(2) (1982), 243–260.

CHAPTER 7

Initial Perspective

A thoughtful man is neither the prisoner of his environment nor the victim of his biography.[1]

It often seems difficult to take a stand, to make a commitment. Maybe that is why people try to avoid taking a position on basic issues. But when you devote the time and energy and take the risks involved in formulating your views, you lay the groundwork for personal and professional growth. By making your perspective on teaching explicit, you can become a more reflective teacher, less likely to be a slave to your unexamined assumptions and more open to change based on your daily experiences.

In previous chapters, you analyzed the situation in which you will teach and examined your past experiences and foundational studies as sources for a perspective on teaching. This chapter helps you to sort out your ideas about teaching and to come to terms with your current perspective.

Sorting Out Ideas

In Chapter 11, you will examine the cooperating teacher's perspective. Perhaps, you will find yourself agreeing with the cooperating teacher. But maybe you would do things differently if you were in charge. An important part of your growth as a teacher will result from your examination of your beliefs about teaching.

One way to sort out ideas is to react to a set of assertions about teaching. Your reactions will help you examine your beliefs on teaching. These beliefs, taken as a whole, constitute your initial perspective.

An instrument provided in Appendix A, the Teacher Belief Inventory (TBI), is designed to help you make your own beliefs about teaching more explicit. Take the time now to complete the TBI. You will use your responses to the statements in it as the basis for further work in this chapter.

Analysis of Beliefs

The TBI consists of 57 items, grouped into the six basic issues introduced in Chapter 5. Each basic issue encompasses between 3 and 21 items in the TBI. For further study, select two or three basic issues or specific aspects of basic issues. It is probably more useful to focus on a small set of issues in depth than to attempt to think through your views on a wide range of issues. In order to make this selection, you might examine your responses to groups of items.

Which groups of items (i.e., issues) were most relevant to your field experience and, therefore, elicited some response?

▶

To which groups of items or issues were your responses most extreme (i.e., a response of 1 or 4)?

▶

To which groups of items or issues did you give a qualified response (i.e., a response of 2 or 3)?

▶

Which issues concern you most?

▶

With this analysis of your responses in mind, you can decide now on which two or three issues you would like to focus your inquiry and explain the reasons behind your choice.

▶

Now you can examine your response to the groups of items you just selected and summarize and elaborate your responses to form a coherent answer to a selected subset of the following questions:

1. Control
   a. How should classroom procedures be determined? (Items 1–5)
   b. How should curriculum and content be determined? (Items 6–15)
   c. How much input should the teachers and parents have regarding the administration of the school? (Items 16–18)
   d. How much control should teachers have over learners' behavior? (Items 19–21)

▶

2. Diversity
   a. How should learners' differences be handled? (Items 22–29)

▶

3. Learning
   a. Is learning facilitated by an individualistic, competitive, or cooperative environment? (Items 30–32)
   b. How does one acquire competence in a subject matter? (Items 33–35)
   c. What is the basis for motivation? (Items 36–37)

▶

4. Teacher's role
   a. How formal a role should a teacher assume? (Items 38–40)

▶

5. School and society
   a. How active should the teacher become in reforming the school and the society? (Items 41–45)
   b. Are schools the cause of social inequalities, or are school problems merely the effects of these societal problems? (Items 46–47)

▶

6. Knowledge
   a. What should be the emphasis of the curriculum? (Items 48–55)
   b. Should different subject matters be kept separate or integrated? (Items 56–57)

▶

For the purpose of future discussions, your responses to the TBI, together with your summary and elaboration of those responses focusing on two or three issues, constitute what we will call your "initial perspective on teaching." This perspective is not considered a general philosophy of teaching but a set of beliefs regarding your specific field experience.

Tracing Origins

We are obviously not born with perspectives on teaching. Where do they come from? By tracing our beliefs back to their origins, we are in a better position to examine their validity. The beliefs become less taken for granted as we identify their sources. We have discussed some of the sources for a perspective in Chapters 4, 5, and 6. Reread your analyses of your experiences as a learner and as a teacher (Chapter 4).

To what extent have these past experiences affected your initial perspective? What other significant experiences have made an impact on your perspective? In what ways?

▶

Did your family's attitude toward teaching or toward education influence your perspective? What about the way you or your brothers and sisters were treated as children by your parents?

▶

What about your professional training? Have the values expressed by faculty members or by your fellow students influenced your perspective? In what ways?

▶

Considering Consequences

The saying "actions speak louder than words" might well have been written to describe the effects of teaching. Any teacher's perspective, if implemented, has consequences for learners. Teachers act in certain ways, based on their beliefs and on contextual constraints, and learners interpret a teacher's actions in both intended and unintended ways. The unintended meanings learners derive from a teacher's actions are part of the school's "hidden curriculum"[2] discussed in Chapter 5. For example, a female teacher in a working-class community school keeps tight control over pupils' classroom behavior, requiring permission before any learner may speak and keeping all children in their seats except when she gives them bathroom passes. She presents the subject matter through a lecture–recitation method, emphasizing rote memorization of the facts as she or the textbook presents them. The children are always kept busy in class, and their homework consists of worksheets with detailed instructions to follow. Promptness, neatness, effort, and compliance with instructions are highly emphasized. The teacher makes a point of publicly displaying the individual pupil's work that most successfully meets these criteria.

Another female teacher works in a school whose community is dominated by the research and development (R&D) division of a large electronics corporation. She allows a great deal of movement in her classroom: Children speak to her and to their classmates without raising hands; different activities are located around the room with children moving from one to another at will; children leave the room to visit the bathroom or learning center without passes. Most of the children engage either in projects during class time with the teacher acting as a resource person, or in small discussion sessions with the teacher acting as a facilitator. Children actively question and criticize sources of information and learn to derive their own conclusions from the available evidence. Independent and logical thinking, problem-solving ability, and creativity seem to be what this teacher looks for in the children's work. Children are encouraged to work cooperatively on the projects they select together and the teacher tries to use inherent interest in projects as the primary motivation.

What might be the differences between the messages that pupils in these two different classrooms receive?

▶

Now apply a similar analysis to your own initial perspective. Try to identify the messages or meanings the learners are likely to take from your beliefs if and when you implement them.[3] Consider both intended and unintended meanings, both short- and long-term effects.

The following sets of questions illustrate this approach to the analysis of your initial perspective for possible consequences. They are only examples. They are grouped according to the same issues presented in Chapter 5 and used to organize the belief inventories in Appendix A.

- *Diversity of learners.* Would you treat different individual or groups of learners differently? Would this differential treatment affect any groups' ability or desire to assume particular social roles in the future?
- *Learning.* Would your emphasis be on the kind of motivation that grades or personal recognition generate, or on the inherent interest learners derive from work they choose to do? What would be the likelihood of the learners' motivation continuing beyond the school years and outside the school walls? How would the learners likely view the subject matter you teach?
- *Role of teacher and control.* What views on authority would the learners likely derive from your role as a teacher and the patterns of control you develop? Would they view authority as arbitrary or reasonable, based on power or on competence, absolute or negotiable?
- *School and society.* From the example you set for the learners, would they be inclined to attempt to change the social order or try to adjust to it? Would they be inclined to participate actively in the political process or to allow others to do it

for them? Would they be inclined to acquiesce to authority or to assess independently the validity of claims?

- *Knowledge.* Would the learners be inclined to view school subject matter as absolute or tentative, value neutral or value laden, useful for interpreting their own everyday experience or primarily for academic matters, comprehensible as an integrated whole or as a set of compartmentalized subjects or topics within subjects?

Although questions such as these are difficult for you to answer before having had a great deal of teaching experience, jot down any answers you can give to any of these questions.

▶

Reread your responses in this section. Do they cause you to reconsider any aspects of your perspective? Write down any reservations you now have about your perspective.

▶

Goals

Chapter 2 discusses the goals or priorities you set for yourself as a *student* teacher. This section will help you use your thinking about your perspective to develop the goals or priorities that you, as a student *teacher*, set for your learners. These latter goals will serve as a guide to your teaching.

Are Goals Necessary?

Education is a purposeful activity. If it has no direction, then it is unlikely to be successful. Without direction, it is even difficult to decide what should count as success.

The same can be said of teaching. One of the major differences between teaching and other interpersonal interactions, such as babysitting, is that teaching has direction. If someone is unable or unwilling to guide an interaction toward some growth or learning, then it is not proper to call that interaction "teaching." Field experiences can be found in many sites: schools, 4-H, Boy Scouts, Girl Scouts, nursing homes, prisons, Big Brother/Big Sister programs, and many more. Whether they count as "teaching" field experiences depends on the appropriateness of someone giving direction or guidance to the interpersonal interaction. In schools, everybody expects the teacher to take responsibility for the learning of the students. In other settings, people may expect or want some degree of "teaching." On the other hand, the situation may call only for a person to be someone's friend or to keep someone company.

To force "teaching" on someone who does not want it in a situation that does not call for it or to avoid the teacher's role when the situation requires it are both common faults of students beginning their initial field experiences. Formulating goals helps teachers decide on the appropriate amount of direction they need to bring to the interactions they have with their clients or pupils.

What Are Some Tentative Goals?

Your initial perspective has already touched on many issues related to goals. By formulating your initial statement of perspective, you were, in part, setting goals for your teaching.

Each dimension—that is, each of the six basic issues—is related to goals of teaching. Each issue raises questions about goals that your perspective might have addressed. By revisiting your perspective, you might gain another basis for revising or expanding your goals.

Control. Who really sets the goals, and who do you think should: the administration, textbook publishers, the state, the cooperating teacher, or you? How sensitive should you be to learner interests?
▶

Diversity. Should you apply the same goals to all the learners, regardless of their backgrounds or abilities?
▶

Teacher's role. Is it important for the learners to develop certain attitudes or feelings toward you as the teacher, such as trust, respect, or honesty?
▶

Learning. Is it important for you to develop a sense of group identity? Should cooperative, competitive, or individualist attitudes be developed? Should you try to develop an interest in the subject matter, and how important is this interest? Should you try to develop a sense of the whole, or should the emphasis be on a set of building blocks of knowledge skills?
▶

Knowledge. What is more important to learn: process-type knowledge (e.g., inquiry, problem solving, and creativity) or content-type knowledge (e.g., facts, concepts, and principles)? Should you help learners to construct their own interpretations of the content or to learn the "accepted" view? Do you want learners to view knowledge as certain or as tentative?
▶

School and society. Are you trying to help the learners adjust to or integrate in the current social order or to provide them "with the knowledge, attitudes, or skills to deal critically and creatively with that reality in order to improve it"?[4]
▶

If you have not done so up to this point, state your goals for the field experience. What do you want to accomplish? In what ways do you intend the field experience to benefit the learner(s)?

Reviewing Goals

You might want to review your goals. For example, you could do the following exercises:

1. Determine whether they are realistic. Can you implement them in this school, with this cooperating teacher?

▶

2. Sort them into short- and long-term goals. For each long-term goal, you could make sure you also have something immediate at which to aim. For each short-term goal, decide if it is an end in itself or a means to an end. If the latter case applies, what is the ultimate end? Was this end included as one of your goals?

▶

3. For each goal, try to identify one or two sample indicators (i.e., things to look for which indicate that the goal is achieved).

▶

4. Next to each goal write 1, 2, or 3 to indicate the priority you assign to it. Let 1 signify that the goal is essential and that you would consider your teaching a failure if it were not largely achieved. Let 2 signify that the goal is very important but that you still would consider your teaching worthwhile for the pupils even if you achieved only partial success toward this goal. Let 3 signify that the goal would be nice to achieve but is far from essential; your success as a teacher does not depend on your success with this goal. Now write down your 1-rated goals here. These will receive the highest priority in your field experience.

▶

Having considered your goals in terms of feasibility, long- and short-term implications, indicators of achievement, and priorities, you might find it necessary to make revisions. If so, do it here.

▶

The goals you have set are only tentative. As you proceed in your field experience, you will undoubtedly have to make midcourse corrections. Goals that initially seem to be straightforward and clearly important may need to be modified or replaced. For example, a learner's math problem may turn out to be a motivational problem, and the teacher would have to adjust goals accordingly.

Not only should goals be modified when necessary, they should also be suspended at times. You should expect to encounter situations in which you need to set aside your goals while you deal with other more pressing problems or capitalize on opportune moments. For example, a teacher may want to postpone teaching how to analyze a poem if the learners just experienced a violent situation in the school, watched a controversial television program, or are excited about an upcoming election.

Goals can guide teaching without placing a stranglehold on it. The key is flexibility in their selection and use.

NOTES

1. George Kelly, *The Psychology of Personal Constructs*, Vol. 2 (New York: Norton, 1955), p. 560.
2. Philip Jackson, *Life in Classrooms* (New York: Holt, Rinehart and Winston, 1968).
3. Carl Grant and Kenneth Zeichner, "On Becoming a Reflective Teacher," in *Preparing for Reflective Teaching*, ed. Carl A. Grant (Boston: Allyn & Bacon, 1984), p. 15.
4. Ibid.

PART THREE

What Is the Situation Where You Will Teach?

CHAPTER 8

The Community and the School

Most people approach social situations with caution. They reserve judgment and commitment until they know something about the individuals and their expectations, the social rules and procedures, and the relation between the specific situation and the larger social context. Most of these factors can be taken for granted in familiar settings, such as college courses or meetings of student activity groups, though every new course or meeting requires a bit of analysis and readjustment. For example, most students spend their first class sessions figuring out what their instructor expects of them. And most freshmen in college spend the entire year figuring out how the whole place works both academically and socially.

In other words, some sort of situation analysis is a necessary part of any social interaction. Because a field experience in teaching is one sort of social interaction, it requires some preliminary analysis of the setting.

This chapter and the next use two types of information for the purpose of analysis: *observations* and *conversations*. Observations can focus on any of the following: (1) the community or neighborhood in which you have your field experiences; (2) the particular school agency or institution, including the physical, social, and personal setting; (3) the room or more generally the space in which you work; (4) the curriculum into which your lessons must fit; (5) the students (or, more generally, the learners) whom you will teach; and (6) the cooperating teacher or co-workers, if any, including their lessons. In addition to observations, conversations with any of the following people could be informative: the cooperating teacher or co-workers (if any); the principal or immediate supervisor of your work (if any); and the learners, clients, or members of the group or family.

If your field experience is done within a school or as a supplement to schooling (e.g., tutoring in school subjects), then you might focus your analysis on the school, the student population, the community, the cooperating teacher, and the classroom. However, if your field experience is done within another context (e.g., a 4-H club or a correctional facility), you will have to adapt Chapters 8 to 11 to the special setting in which you will teach. In doing so, you will find ideas in these four chapters that you can modify for your purposes. For example, if you serve as a co-leader of 4-H, the other co-leader is not a cooperating teacher, but much of what we discuss about cooperating teachers applies equally well to co-leaders.

This chapter focuses only on the analysis of the school and the community. The next chapter examines the classroom and the curriculum.

The Community

The classroom is a society in miniature. This minisociety reflects in part the society in which the school exists. Children often act and interact in certain ways because they see their parents and friends do so. If they experience anti-intellectualism, materialism, conformity, or prejudice at home or at their neighbors' houses, they are likely to demonstrate these tendencies at school. If their parents and neighbors support the school's efforts, place a high priority on achievement, and are courteous and well mannered, the children are likely to be similarly inclined in school. It is therefore important to find out about the community from which the learners come and in which the school is situated. Although interviews with parents and community members are obviously desirable, they are typically not feasible.

EXERCISE 8.1

Analysis of the Community

Here are some things you can do to learn about the community:

1. Read a local newspaper every day for several weeks. Pay particular attention to news stories, editorials, and letters to the editor concerning the schools.
   a. Is the community proud of its schools? What do they seem to be most proud of? The athletic teams? The band? Scholarship winners? Innovations? Efforts to cut the budget? Improved test scores? The buildings?
   b. What makes people angry? Liberal policies? Conservative policies? Indecision? Political heavy-handedness? Permissiveness? Vandalism?
   c. Read non-education-related items. How diverse is the community? Ethnically? In terms of religious practices? In terms of socioeconomic status?
   d. Where do people work, and what do they spend their leisure time doing?

▶

▶

▶

▶

   Write a brief description of the community and its attitude toward the schools, as reflected by the newspaper.

▶

2. Walk around the neighborhood of the school, looking at the houses, businesses, and people on the street. Go to a local establishment near the school building, perhaps a barber shop, restaurant, bar, or self-service laundry. If asked about yourself, mention that you will be working at the school soon and note the reaction. Sympathy? Admiration? Suspicion? Listen to conversations or start one. What do the people think about the job the schools are doing? What do they think about young people today? What is first and foremost on their minds? Property taxes? Deterioration of the neighborhood? Permissiveness? Vandalism?

EXERCISE 8.1 Continued

Busing? Write a brief description of the neighborhood, its inhabitants, and their attitude toward the schools as you find it reflected in these experiences.

▶

Perhaps the school draws students from several neighborhoods. How do these neighborhoods contrast?

▶

Compare your two descriptions. Do they conflict or do they complement one another? If they conflict, how can you reconcile them? Does the newspaper really reflect the local neighborhood? Did you read enough of it? Were you exposed to enough community members to get an accurate picture?

▶

Now try to draw some implications from this study for the school and classroom. To do this, make some predictions of what you might find in the school. What sorts of careers are likely to be most and least highly prized? How much value is likely to be placed on proper dress for the pupils and for the teachers? How cautious are the teachers likely to be with regard to discussing controversial issues in the classroom? How much support from the parents are teachers likely to get when they discipline students?

▶

The School

Schools are both similar and different. Compared with hospitals and churches, schools in general are distinctive and highly uniform. But within this relative uniformity, there are significant differences or variations on a theme. And just as with faces, the more one comes to know schools, the more one becomes sensitive to the differences. Some teem with activity. Others are as hushed as libraries. Some are colorful and stimulate the senses. Others are dull and drab. In some, long, straight corridors dominate the architecture. In others, open spaces are common. Some school groups resemble country clubs, whereas others resemble prisons. What accounts for the differences in atmosphere and what effect do these differences have on the people who function there?

EXERCISE 8.2

A Walk Around the School

Take a walk around the school, both inside and out (remember to have the permission of the principal). Here are some things to which you might want to pay particular attention:

1. *The halls.* Who is in the halls during class time? Teachers? The principal? Students? Do the students you find have hall passes? Where are they going?

▶

(continued)

EXERCISE 8.2 **Continued**

▶ Look at the walls. Are they used for displays of any kind? If so, is it student work? Commercially prepared displays? Are they at eye level for children? What subject matter is represented? Any announcements or bulletin boards? What is on them?

▶ What is the noise level, and what kind of noise is it? Laughter? Yelling? A "hum of activity"? Hammering and other construction noises? Teachers' voices?

▶ Are the halls littered? How much pride in the school is evidenced?

2. *The library (learning center).* Is it an inviting place? Do you find it a comfortable environment for reading? Browsing?

   What is the noise level? Hushed silence? Outbursts of laughter? Are there distractions? Is the atmosphere serious or silly? Stiff or relaxed?

   What is the attitude of the teacher in charge? Does he or she act more as a resource person or as a warden?

   Are students there by choice or by assignment? Do they come with or without passes? Is coming to the library viewed more as a privilege or as a necessary task?

▶

EXERCISE 8.3

A Conversation with the Principal

You might get an opportunity to talk with the principal. If you do, here are some suggestions that will increase your understanding of the school and, particularly, the principal's role in it.

Curriculum

Ask the principal about the school's objectives and curriculum. Is there a state curriculum? Try to acquire a copy. Under what objectives does the school operate? Are there objectives that the school as a whole tries to achieve? Are there particular objectives for each grade level and/or each subject? How and by whom were these developed? Who selected the textbooks and programs in use? How were they selected?

▶

Multicultural Aspects

Ask the principal about the ethnic, racial, religious, and socioeconomic backgrounds of the students in the school. How diverse is the student population? What minority groups in the community seem most concerned about the school's ability to provide an appropriate education for their children? How would he or she describe the experience of minorities in the

EXERCISE 8.3 Continued

school? Can he or she think of any exceptions to this generality? What are the school's expectations for each of the minority groups? Are any of the groups under- or overrepresented in remedial classes, programs for the gifted and talented, or in the upper or lower tracks (if the school is tracked)? If so, why?

▶

Organization and Schedule

Ask the principal about the size of the school, the number of teachers, and the size of classes. On this last matter, ask about the average size class and the range of class sizes within the school. Ask to see a copy of the "master schedule." With this schedule in hand ask the principal or try to determine from the schedule the number of planning and preparation periods, as well as the number of nonteaching duties (e.g., cafeteria duty) for each teacher. If this is a secondary school, notice the number of preparations (i.e., different courses) for each teacher and the number of teachers in each department. This schedule will also tell you the length of each period and the number of class periods each day. Ask the principal about the number of tracks, ability groups, or levels at which courses are offered. If this is an elementary school, try to determine whether there is a school-wide uniformity with regard to scheduling language arts and math, or if this is a matter for each teacher to determine. Notice on the schedule at what grades subjects begin to become departmentalized, that is, when students go to a different teacher for a particular subject. Ask the principal about "pull-outs." Approximately how many children in each class are "pulled out" of their regular class for special help? And how many special services are provided through the use of pull-outs? Are there any times during the day when no pull-outs occur? Are any special services provided in the regular classroom? Finally, ask the principal about ability grouping within the classrooms. How many reading groups are used at each grade level? Are any other subjects ability grouped?

▶

Rules and Discipline

What are the school's rules, and how is discipline handled? Is there a printed set of rules of conduct? If not, what are they? What infractions are the most serious and what are the penalties? What is the frequency of infractions? Who is supposed to deal with each type of infraction? When should an infraction be handled entirely within the classroom? When and how should the principal (or vice principal) be involved? When and how should parents be involved?

▶

Leadership Style

Try to determine from the principal's remarks whether he or she is more of a manager or an instructional leader. The former tries to keep a school running smoothly and efficiently. The latter tries to stimulate innovation, to encourage thought and debate, to keep teachers' minds active, and even to set an example as a continuously growing and expanding professional. Obviously, the two types of principals have very different approaches to controversy, disruptions, noise, etc. Clearly, the kind of teacher you are encouraged to be will differ depending on the atmosphere established by different principals.

▶

EXERCISE 8.4

A Visit to the Faculty Room

If you go to the faculty room for a cup of coffee, listen to the types of conversations going on. Here are some things to notice: How old are the teachers in the room? What subjects are discussed? Are they related or not related to school? What outside activities predominate? Sports? Politics? Social events? What school-related matters predominate? Classroom problems? Concern for particular pupils? The administration? Other teachers? Parents? School sports? When discussion is on a particular student, does the talk reflect disgust, respect, hope, or despair for the student? How do the teachers dress?

▶

At this point, it might be worthwhile to summarize your conclusions about the school and its staff. What is its philosophy of teaching? Do you agree with it? What sorts of problems might you encounter working there?

▶

The information you have collected using this chapter as a guide will help you better understand what it might be like to teach in this school. Each school has a character of its own; some even go so far as to call it a *culture*.[1] Take the time to write down your conclusions from this analysis. What aspects of the community and the school are you most excited about?

▶

What aspects of the community and school are most concerning to you?

▶

Action Research

After observing the school community and collecting information, you will have a better understanding of the possibilities and problems facing it. At this point, you may choose to explore further the opportunities you have discovered, or you might decide to work on a solution to one or more problems you have come across. In the past 15 years, a growing number of teachers have started looking into action research as a useful approach to help the school community solve many of the problems it faces each day.

Action research is the systematic investigation of a community that involves the subjects within the community as active participants in the research. Teachers undertaking community action research in the school or classroom assume that members of the community will collaborate as equal partners in the research because it is assumed that members of a group will wish to better understand any problems they face and also want to be part of the solution.

Action research, like other forms of research, includes four defining tasks:

- Identifying a problem or issue to research
- Following a method of investigation

- Offering an analysis of the problem or issue that leads to better understanding
- Developing a plan of action

As you spend more time in school, you will see areas in need of improvement. Action research has been described as giving teachers opportunities to focus on finding solutions to classroom and school problems or improving one's own teaching practice.[2]

How might you apply action research in your teaching? It is routinely used to identify and provide answers to problems such as:

- Why several students are consistently not engaged in the lessons
- Why you lose control of the class after lunch each day
- How to effectively communicate with uncooperative parents
- How to better differentiate learning activities in your teaching
- What type of assessment works best with your class

There are several approaches to conducting action research once you have identified a general issue or problem. A simple action research routine is outlined below to present the basic features of this methodology. Ernest Stringer's model of the action research process has three phases—Look, Think, and Act:[3]

Look	Gather data
	Define and describe the situation
Think	Analyze
	Theorize
Act	Plan
	Implement
	Evaluate

Let's examine the three stages in more detail so you can begin to see how you might use action research in your own teaching or field experience. According to Stringer, the purpose of the Look phase is to gather enough information so that you can begin to understand the perspectives of the participants in the research. You can gather information through:

- Interviews
- Surveys
- Focus groups
- Observation
- Questionnaires

It is important to ensure that interviews, surveys, and questionnaires ask questions that do not lead the participants in a certain direction or impose your perspective. The interview questions should be neutral and open ended. For example, if you are interviewing a student about motivation in the classroom, you should pose a question that allows the participant to frame the response and speak from experience. "Tell me how you spend a typical day in the classroom?" is neutral and open ended. "Tell me why you find school boring?" is a leading question that frames the response for the participant.

Each survey question should be focused on a single issue (e.g., "Are you comfortable letting students use calculators during a math exam?"). Surveys should not include several issues within one question (e.g., "Are you comfortable letting students use calculators and open books during exams?").

Observations should include note-taking that both describes and interprets. Rudimentary notes taken while observing a kindergarten reading circle might describe the event as "6 children, 4 girls and 2 boys, were sitting in a semi-circle on the floor in front of the teacher, who read *Frog and Toad* from 11:15 to 11:30." When observing, you should make sure to include detailed notes on the people, environment, activities, actions, objects, and feelings that occur during the time you are there. For example, the same event could also be described as, "6 children were listening to the teacher read *Frog and Toad*. 3 of the girls seemed bored, and the teacher was probably worried about the timing of the lesson because he kept looking nervously at the clock."

After gathering data, you enter the Think phase, where you analyze the information you have collected. You need to organize the data and information you have collected before interpreting. Now is the time to categorize the information. As you read through your data, you can begin coding and separating the ideas, issues, and events into larger units of meaning. If you find terms, such as *leader, leading, manager,* and *person in charge* recurring in your data, then after coding, you can place these references together under the category "Leadership." After you have created themes, you need to go back to the participants with your interpretations and discuss their interpretations of the same data. Allowing all stakeholders to participate extends analysis and builds a sense of community. You now can enter the part of the Think phase in which you "enrich" the analysis through one of several accepted frameworks, including concept mapping, interpretive questions, problem analysis, and organizational review. After you refine the analysis, you can organize and present a collaborative report.

The final phase, Act, involves planning, implementing, and evaluating the research. As you enter the planning phase, you need to identify the goals, resources, and people needed to carry out the action plan that you have developed. After planning, you need to implement the plan, which requires communicating with all participants, as well as assisting and linking individuals in order to systematically put your plans into action. Finally, you and the participants can evaluate the plan after implementation to assess strengths and weaknesses and perhaps revise it as you continue to work on making the school an effective and productive environment.

Although this is only a brief introduction to action research, you now have a basic understanding of the goals and possible applications that can be used to enhance your teaching. Keep in mind that the objective of action research is to improve the learning and teaching you are involved in, as well as your environment; it is therefore important to involve the people you work with—teachers, students, staff, guardians, and parents—in order to gather and interpret as much information as you need to bring about intentional and constructive change.

NOTES

1. See Michael Fullan, *The New Meaning of Educational Change*, 2nd ed. (New York: Teacher's College Press, 1991); Seymour B. Sarason, *The Culture of the School and the Problem of Change*, 2nd ed. (Boston: Allyn & Bacon, 1982).
2. James H. McMillan, *Educational Research: Fundamentals for the Consumer* (Boston: Allyn & Bacon, 2004).
3. Ernest T. Stringer, *Action Research*, 3rd ed. (Thousand Oaks, CA: Sage Publications, 2007).

CHAPTER 9

The Classroom, Technology, and the Curriculum*

As Lortie mentions, "The average student has spent 13,000 hours in direct contact with classroom teachers by the time he or she graduates from high school."[1] Lortie calls this contact "apprenticeship by observation."[2] There are definite limits to this type of apprenticeship, however:

> The student is the "target" of teacher efforts and sees the teacher front stage and center like an audience viewing a play. Students do not receive invitations to watch the teacher's performance from the wings; they are not privy to the teacher's private intentions and personal reflections on classroom events. Students rarely participate in selecting goals, making preparations, or postmortem analyses. Thus they are not pressed to place the teacher's actions in a pedagogically oriented framework. They are witnesses from their own student-oriented perspectives. . . . What students learn about teaching, then, is intuitive and imitative rather than explicit and analytical; it is based on individual personalities rather than pedagogical principles.[3]

Students, then, should be expected to know no more about teaching than an avid moviegoer knows about directing or a dance buff knows about choreography. One of the tasks of this chapter will be to unlearn (but not to forget) the student perspective as one step toward becoming a teacher. As Walker and Adelman state:

> The teacher sees the class quite differently from the way it is seen by a child. Children are faced with the problem of either producing a performance that the teacher requires, or reacting against it in some way. In either event, a major element in the classroom situation for the pupils is what they take to be the demands of the teacher, whether these are stated or unstated. For them the situation is inevitably one of constraint.[4]

For the teacher, the problem is quite different: The teacher's task is to get beyond the constraints as rapidly as possible; he or she has to define the situation and set the pace—to make sure that what he or she wants to happen seems to happen.

For many people starting teaching, it comes as a shock to realize that the spotlight is on them, that the initiative is in their hands, that they suddenly have responsibility for what happens and what might happen. The classroom, which they saw previously as an unshakable social structure, suddenly becomes bewildering and problematic, fraught with difficulties at every turn. Many consequently exaggerate in their minds the degree to which the situation is "out of control" simply because they are unaware

*Written with Aram deKoven.

of the change in perspective brought about by the shift from the back to the front of the class.[5]

Thus, seeing the teacher and the classroom differently is the main task here. Whereas Chapter 8 focuses on the school as a whole, this chapter examines the particular classroom or setting in which you will work. Whereas Chapter 8 helped you to see the school from the faculty's, the principal's, and the typical student's perspective, this chapter helps you understand what dilemmas and tasks the teacher faces and what the teacher does to cope with them. Chapter 10 helps you look at the particular students you will be teaching.

Thinking in terms of frames (mentioned in Chapter 6), you may think of the community as forming a frame within which schools operate. Schools, in turn, form another frame within which classrooms operate. Classrooms, too, form a frame within which teaching occurs, and it is that innermost frame we consider here.

The Classroom

Teachers try to provide environments for learning. The environment includes a physical dimension and an interpersonal dimension. In order to understand the resources and constraints within which the classroom operates and the way the classroom layout reflects the teacher's personal perspective, we will begin our analysis of the classroom by examining the physical layout.

EXERCISE **9.1**

Classroom Map

One way to analyze the classroom layout is to make a sketch, roughly to scale. Here are some things to include and label, if present:

- Doors and windows
- Desks, tables, and chairs
- Bookcases, cabinets, and display cases
- Closets and other storage areas
- Sinks and lavatories
- Adjoining rooms or hallways
- Blackboards, projectors, screens
- Special resource areas (e.g., math table, reading corner)
- Computers
  (Use a separate sheet of paper for your map.)

In addition, you might want to note the following features of the classroom:

1. *Walls.* Describe color. What posters, pictures, wall charts, exhibits, or notices are there? How long have they been there? Do they look as though they are still being used by someone?
2. *Vantage point.* Do any other parts of the school overlook the room? Does the room look out on the outside world?
3. *Furniture.* Does the furniture arrangement appear more conducive to cooperative, competitive, or individualistic work? How flexible does the arrangement appear? In what condition is the furniture? Has it been abused?
4. *Equipment.* What kinds of equipments are there? How accessible is it? What condition is it in? Does it look as though it is seldom, occasionally, or frequently used? And by whom is it used, the teacher or the learners?
5. *Bulletin boards.* What are they used for? Who uses them (the teacher, the learners, or the administration)? How recently were they changed?

EXERCISE **9.1** Continued

6. *Specialization.* Are there areas in the room used for special purposes? Is specialization by school subject (e.g., math area), by topic or unit (e.g., space travel), or by learning mode (e.g., audio tutorial)?
7. *Atmosphere.* Note the room's temperature, air circulation and ventilation, smells, lighting (artificial and natural) and glare, acoustics (echoes and resonance), outside noise (e.g., traffic), and furniture noise.

General comments: What are your general impressions of this room? Is it crowded, cluttered, or comfortable? Is it boring and bland or stimulating? How would you like to spend six hours a day here? If you had not met or observed the teacher, from what you have noted about the classroom, what might you assume about the teacher's approach to teaching?

▶

Technology

The presence in classrooms of electronic instructional technologies has grown tremendously in the past decade. In 2001, Internet-connected computers were found in more than 99.5 percent of schools and 87 percent of K through 12 classrooms.[6] The breadth of this change is incredible; both students and teachers are now able to connect to other students and teachers around the globe in an instant. Never before has so much information about so many subjects been this readily accessible to so many students. Computers can help young students research, prepare, and present their work in ways previously thought possible only for professionals. Overall, the presence of technology in the classroom has helped the processes of education and learning.

However, these advances do come with drawbacks. Not all of the information we can find on the Internet is equally valid. As a result, teachers, parents, and volunteers like you need to encourage young people not only to take the initiative in seeking out answers to their questions but also to be critical of the source or sources of the information they gather. Being critical of the sources of information can be a daunting proposal for a young person. We adults may have to bear some of the blame for this, since many of us tell children or have told children over the years to "just do as you are told!" To a young person, questioning the sources of information may be tantamount to questioning the authority of adults, which many young people are reluctant to do. On the Internet, much bad information is placed in close proximity to good information. For this reason, we need to teach youths to be critical of the sources of the information they take as fact, even if that means we also encourage them to question us about the things we tell them.

Issues surrounding computers and other technologies in school classrooms are in fact complex. On the surface, we might expect that the presence of computers and Internet connections in the classroom would make schools more efficient and productive, that they would make teaching and learning more exciting, and that they would better help prepare youths for the jobs of the future. To this end, schools, businesses, and communities have invested tremendous sums of money in equipping classrooms with computers and other high-tech gadgetry. Cuban, among others, feels this investment has been far too great, with too few measurable benefits. The reality is that in classrooms around the nation, new technology has been largely underutilized, and it has not done much to enhance learning or teaching.[7] Computers in the classroom can certainly, under the right situations, help students as they navigate their way through school. However, investments in computers and other technologies should never be allowed to trump or act as a substitute for good, caring, and committed teachers working with well-thought-out curricula in carefully designed spaces.

EXERCISE 9.2

Technology Issues

For educators and administrators, the presence of computers in the classroom brings up many critical issues. As a volunteer placed in a classroom, what would you do in the following situations? Write down how you would handle these short scenarios and share your responses with your classmates.

Issues of Censorship

You discover that some of your students are using the computer to look at websites that deny the existence of the Holocaust and propagate messages of hate. You find the material objectionable but wonder to yourself if this isn't the right of your students to look at what they want to. Barring the presence of school policies specifically addressing this issue, what would you do? What would you say to the youths looking at this website? What other lessons about Internet use can be taught using this example?

▶

Issues of Safety

You discover a group of girls using the computer to instant message another computer user. You overhear them sending their names and addresses over the Internet and then attempting to set up a face-to-face meeting with the other instant messenger (who claims to be a 15-year-old boy). Why is this potentially dangerous? What do you do about this? Are you trampling on these girls' right to free speech?

▶

Issues of Monitoring

A group of seventh-grade students are huddled around the computer, and they are acting giddy. You peer over their shoulders and discover that they are looking at pictures of female genitalia. You proceed to scare the youngsters away from the machine and then sit down at the terminal to discover that the website that they were viewing was not a pornographic site but rather a website geared toward disseminating information to youths about sexually transmitted diseases. Barring the presence of school policies specifically forbidding looking at sites of this nature, what would you do about this situation? What would you say to these youths looking at this website? Should young people be able to get information about health from the Internet, even if some of the information includes pictures of sexual organs? For you, where does the line blur between what is educational material and what is age-inappropriate material for youths to be viewing?

▶

Equity Issues

Students in your class hand in to you projects that are all nicely done, with color photographs, fancy graphics, and eye-catching fonts. Two students hand in papers that are not done on computers and look less polished. These students come to talk with you and complain that they could not do as good a job because they do not have computers at home. The material, however, on these less polished projects is solid. Do you take this into consideration for grading purposes? What do you do with or say to young people whose families cannot afford computers? Should you adjust for these differences when grading students' work?

▶

The Curriculum

Using the idea of frames within frames mentioned earlier in this chapter, the curriculum functions as a frame within which teachers plan lessons. Sometimes, these curricular frames are school district-wide, sometimes they are school-wide, and occasionally, they are unique to a particular classroom.

EXERCISE 9.3

Curriculum Analysis

What you see taking place when you observe a teacher teaching a lesson is part of a larger story. Before examining one particular scene of the drama—that is, a lesson—it is useful to examine the entire script. In this way, you will gain an understanding of the teacher's reasons for choosing to teach a particular lesson in a particular way, both in terms of where the teacher is going with the lesson and where the learners have already come from. It is for this reason that some analysis of the teacher's curriculum is important as you reflect on what you see and hear in the classroom or whatever is the setting for the lesson. If there is a document the teacher uses to guide his or her daily planning, ask to see it. This document may or may not be called the *curriculum*. It may instead be called the *syllabus*, the *scope and sequence*, the *leader's guide*, or the *teacher's guide*. For teachers who teach strictly by the book, you may only be able to find a textbook. Once you obtain one or more documents, the teacher uses as a basis for planning, try to answer the following questions:

1. What seems to be the underlying philosophy that guides the general approach? You might want to refer to the discussion of the six basic issues (Chapter 5) as a source of ideas in this inquiry. Often, curriculum documents do not make their basic philosophical commitments explicit, leaving the teacher in the position of reading between the lines. The sections about learning and motivation, the role of the teacher, and knowledge will likely be the most relevant to this search for a philosophy.

    ▶

2. What appear to be the curriculum's educational goals and objectives? That is, what are the intended characteristics of learners who complete the entire curriculum? Consider both their general characteristics and more specific learning outcomes. Examples of the former include goals, such as becoming more tolerant of people who are different and becoming more scientifically and mathematically literate. Examples of the latter include knowledge and skills, such as knowing about specific contributions made by particular ethnic groups and being able to calculate the slope of a straight-line graph.

    ▶

3. What seem to be the general beliefs about the best methods of teaching? Is the expected role of the teacher a transmitter of information, a group facilitator, a resource person, a source of intellectual stimulation, a coach, a social worker or counselor, a task master, or some other role? What roles are learners expected to play?

    ▶

4. What does the curriculum appear to count as success in teaching, and how (if at all) does the curriculum suggest that learning should be evaluated? Is success to be judged by evidence on paper-and-pencil tests or by performance of real-world tasks?

    ▶

EXERCISE 9.4

Lesson Profile[8]

Like a piece of music, a good lesson can have different "movements" which have various, contrasting moods, but which, taken together as a sequence, form a cumulative experience.[9]

With a basic familiarity of the classroom layout, you are equipped to observe the class in action. A useful way to begin is by making a lesson profile of one or two lessons (i.e., class periods). Think of a lesson as a sequence of events; there is a beginning, a middle, and an end. The beginning might consist of a settling-down period, a preface and/or introduction, or the presentation of instructions for the main activity. The middle might entail a demonstration, lecture, film, discussion, presentation of work by groups, set work, or any combination of these and other activities. The end might be used as a period for summary, conclusions, cleaning up, homework assignments, or test taking, among other things. You might list the sequence of events that took place during the lesson, indicating the approximate length of time each event required, and describing what seem to you to be important aspects of each. You might want to include information about some of the following for each event:

- Activity of teacher (what is the teacher doing?)
- Activity of learners (what are the learners doing?)
- Resources (what resources are utilized?)
- Noise level (high, moderate, low)
- Use of space (what areas of the classroom are used?)
- Concentration level (high, moderate, low)
- Movement of learners
- Movement of teacher
- Number of learners involved
- Lines of communication (teacher to student, student to teacher, student to student)

There are, of course, other aspects you might want to use. Feel free to improvise. (Use a separate sheet of paper for your lesson profile.)

After completing a lesson profile, consider asking to see the teacher's lesson plan, if one exists. Compare the plan with the profile.

What, if any, tentative conclusions do you have regarding this teacher's perspective? For example:

1. How responsive does the teacher appear to be to moods or interests of the learners? To what extent does any discrepancy between the lesson plan and the profile represent the responsiveness of the teacher?
2. Does the teacher treat different learners differently in terms of grouping, time allocation, tasks, standards, etc.?
3. How much of the lesson is done by learners individually and how much in groups? Is there a spirit of competition or cooperation in the groups? Does the teacher say or do anything to encourage or discourage this spirit?
4. How formal/informal does the teacher appear to be? What does the teacher do to develop or reinforce this role?
5. What seems to be the point of the lesson? For example, is it to memorize some material, share some ideas, find some "correct" answers or procedures, check to see if the learners have been doing their work, or to clarify ideas? How does the teacher communicate the intent to the class?

▶

EXERCISE 9.5

Analysis of Lesson Elements

You can take your observation one step further by applying a template to the lesson—that is, looking for a set of basic elements. For our present purposes, we will consider a relatively simple and straightforward approach to the analysis of lessons, adapted from the work of Hunter.[10] Hunter provides an outline of the basic elements of a lesson, which can function as a set of questions to answer as you observe the teacher in action:

1. *Anticipatory set.* What has the teacher done to get the students' attention, to relate the lesson to what the students have done previously, and to engage them in the lesson? Look for how the teacher communicates to students that the lesson is about to begin, whether the teacher reviews previous lessons, how the teacher tries to stimulate interest, and what the teacher does to lay the groundwork for the lesson.

   ▶

2. *Objective and purpose.* What has the teacher done to communicate to the students what they are supposed to get out of the lesson and why that is important?

   ▶

3. *Input.* What knowledge and skills necessary to achieve the lesson's objective does the teacher make available to the students, and how does the teacher provide them? Look for the specific methods employed, whether they include lecture, discussion, laboratory, seatwork, or some other method.

   ▶

4. *Modeling.* How does the teacher show the students what they are expected to produce or learn to do? What kinds of examples and demonstrations are employed?

   ▶

5. *Checking for understanding.* How does the teacher monitor the students' understanding of concepts and proficiency in skills during the lesson? How does the teacher adjust the lesson on the basis of this feedback? Look for the ways in which the teacher invites questions, how the teacher asks and answers questions (including the amount of time the teacher waits for an answer), how many and what type of students the teacher involves in questioning, and what the teacher does with a student's answer, especially when it is incorrect.

   ▶

6. *Guided practice.* How does the teacher give the students opportunities to practice using their new knowledge or skill under direct teacher supervision?

   ▶

7. *Independent practice.* How does the teacher provide opportunities for students to practice using their new knowledge or skills independently after the teacher is reasonably sure that students will not make serious errors?

   ▶

(continued)

EXERCISE 9.5 Continued

As Hunter points out, a common error in the observation of teaching is the belief that "all good things must be in every lesson."[11] The teacher must decide which of the elements to include, as well as how to include them. The advantage of templates like Hunter's is that they give us things to look for; the disadvantage is that such a template is not appropriate for every lesson. Figuring out why particular elements are absent from a lesson can provide important insights into teaching.

The classroom and the curriculum used by the teacher function as both resources and constraints for your teaching. As resources, they provide a structure within which you can work and a set of ideas, materials, equipment, and spaces that you can utilize for your lessons. As constraints, they limit what you can teach and how you can teach it. Whatever you do in the classroom will have to fit into an existing curricular and classroom framework.

A glass is both half empty and half full, depending on how you want to look at it. Whether you choose to consider the classroom and the curriculum as resources or constraints, it should be clear that you will need to understand how they function. Take the time now to jot down any thoughts you might have about these two important aspects of teaching that you will want to consider as you plan your teaching.

▶

With these thoughts in mind, it is time to consider the most significant factor affecting what and how you teach: the students.

NOTES

1. Dan Lortie, *Schoolteacher* (Chicago: University of Chicago Press, 1975), p. 61.
2. Ibid.
3. Ibid., p. 62.
4. Rob Walker and Clem Adelman, *A Guide to Classroom Observation* (London: Methuen, 1975).
5. Ibid., p. 8.
6. National Center for Educational Statistics, *Internet Access in U.S. Public Schools and Classrooms: 1994–2001.* Retrieved December 11, 2002, from http://nces.ed.gov/pubs2002/internet/.
7. Larry Cuban, *Oversold and Underused: Computers in the Classroom* (Cambridge, MA: Harvard University Press, 2001).
8. Adapted from Walker and Adelman, *A Guide to Classroom Observation.*
9. Ibid., p. 25.
10. Madeline Hunter, "Knowing, Teaching and Supervising," in *Using What We Know about Teaching,* ed. Philip Hosford (Alexandria, VA: Association for Supervision and Curriculum Development, 1984), pp. 169–192.
11. Ibid., p. 176.

CHAPTER 10

The Students*

Our memories are remarkably short. It was not very long ago that you were a student in elementary school. Yet most college students have difficulty seeing school and teachers in the same way school-age children do. And the younger the schoolchildren, the greater the gap between your perspectives and theirs. Nevertheless, one of the most valuable things teachers can possess is an understanding of how their students view themselves and the school. With this understanding, we are in a better position to appreciate the way students experience school and how our teaching affects that experience.

Clearly, school is not just the building and the teachers within it; school is also (and, perhaps, more significantly for children) a place to interact with other children. That is, school is a social experience. Therefore, we are interested not only in the students' backgrounds and interests but also in the ways the students regard one another, the ways they interact within groups, and the ways groups of children interact. In short, we are also interested in learning about the student culture.

Students in the School

By studying the students, you can find out the composition of the student population and what it is like being a student in a particular school. These two aspects of school life are best identified through a combination of talks with and observations of the students. Here are some suggestions.

EXERCISE **10.1**

Conversations with Students in the School

During recesses and lunchtime, or after school, try to talk with at least one student. You might want to tell the student that you are not reporting to anybody, you just want to find out about the school where you will be working.

You might ask about the student's neighborhood. Are the people there like the people in the school? How are they different?

What does the student want to do after leaving school? Has he or she made any plans? If the student is old enough, ask if he or she works after school hours or during vacations.

(continued)

---

*Written with Aram deKoven.

EXERCISE 10.1 Continued

Does the student like school? What about it does he or she like and dislike? What is the student's favorite subject? What about it does he or she like? Ask similar questions about the subject the student dislikes the most and the subjects in which the student does the best and the worst. What about extracurricular activities, including sports?

Who is the student's favorite teacher this year? Who is the favorite teacher of all time? Would most others agree? What makes this teacher the best? You might try to identify the characteristics of this student's "ideal" teacher.

Who are the student's friends? Is this student in a clique? If so, what is it like? Who in the school does he or she like or dislike? What does he or she like or dislike about these kids? Whose opinion really counts?

Are there kids in the school who are "different"? What makes them "different"? How does this student feel about kids who are "different"?

How much help does this student receive from his or her parents? What kind of help? With homework or projects? Moral support? Has this student ever been in trouble in school? What kind? How did the parents react? What does the school do when kids cause trouble?

After talking to a few students, try to summarize your notes here, comparing and contrasting the students' backgrounds, goals and aspirations, likes and dislikes, ideal teacher, friendship groups, attitudes about people who are "different," and the role of their parents in their schooling.

Backgrounds:
▶

Goals and aspirations:
▶

Likes and dislikes:
▶

Ideal teacher:
▶

Friendship groups and "significant others":
▶

Attitudes about people who are "different":
▶

Parents' role:
▶

EXERCISE 10.2

Observing Students in the School

Try to observe some students. The cafeteria during lunch and the playground or school grounds during recess are possible places.

1. *Dress.* How are the children dressed? Comment on neatness and apparent affluence. Also note differences in dress among groups of children.

2. *Language.* What is students' out-of-class language like? How is it different from their in-class language? What sorts of emotions do they express with their language? Do they use abusive language? Note differences in languages among groups of children. Do some groups use language as a code to keep their members separated from other groups?

3. *Interests.* If you are unobtrusive, you will be able to overhear fragments of conversations. What do the children talk about? Teachers? Sports and cars? Grades? The opposite sex? Clothes? Current events? Tests? Note differences in topics of conversation for different groups. Do some groups talk about other groups?

4. *Groups.* What groups can you identify? (Groups are particularly noticeable in secondary schools.) Some groups you might notice are "jocks," "druggies," "skaters," "snobs," "nerds," "preppies," and students of various racial or ethnic backgrounds. How would you characterize each group? Consider dress, language, race, interests, how physical, materialistic, and so on. How rigid is group definition? That is, are some students members of more than one group? Or do some members of groups mix with members of other groups? Are there loners? What are their characteristics?

5. *Territory.* Does each of the groups have its own "territory"? Which one has the most territory? The least territory? How closely guarded is each group's territory?

6. *Conflict.* What sorts of conflict do you observe? Are the protagonists members of different groups? What is the source of the conflict (e.g., physical or verbal abuse, invasion of one group's territory by another)? How is the conflict settled (if at all) and by whom?

7. *Dominance and power.* Do any of the groups appear to be dominant? Which are the most and the least powerful groups? What is the source of each group's power (e.g., academic skills, athletic skill, muscle, "street knowledge")? Do any of the groups depend on adult approval for their power?

Summarize what you have observed about the students in the school. Who are they and what is it like to "live" in this school?

▶

Students in the Classroom

"Every person is unique." Although most teachers would agree with this statement, they tend to talk about student types (e.g., slow learners, underachievers, disadvantaged, at risk, science oriented, jocks, college bound). This tendency is understandable in all people when they try to reduce the complexity of a situation. Typing students transforms a room filled with 35 unique individuals to one with 3, 5, or even 10 types of students. But, however understandable or natural this tendency, it is also potentially dangerous, because such a practice might blind teachers to their students' individuality. This is why you should get to know your students as individuals. Each has particular strengths and weaknesses, likes and dislikes, and desirable and undesirable traits. Not only is each student an individual, but each is also a member of one or more friendship groups. Understanding who a student looks to for approval or respect is also of vital importance.

The first step in getting acquainted with the students is to observe them in class. Here is one approach to observing students.

EXERCISE 10.3

Who Are the Students in the Classroom?[1]

Stand as unobtrusively as possible in the classroom before any students arrive. Jot down notes as they begin to arrive. Some suggestions are as follows:

1. Notice who arrives first and last.
2. How many and of what age and gender are the students in this class?
3. Do students remain in the same groups inside the classroom as those in which they arrived?
4. Look at the overall spacing between groups. Is it uniform? Does it reflect furniture, resource location, or friendship groups? Are there any cliques?
5. Who are the isolates?
6. How much movement between groups occurs? Note how changes in groupings occur during the day or class period.
7. What roles do particular students play? For example, who is the joker, the cynic, the teacher's pet, the introvert, etc.?
8. Which students raise their hands most often and least often (or never) when the teacher asks a question?
9. Which students does the teacher never call on?
10. Is the behavior of the students who sit in the back of the room different from that of the rest of the class? What about the corners, the middle, and the front?
11. Which students seem to be paying the most and the least attention, and what is the range of attention spans?
12. Which students ask for most help and whom do they ask (the teacher, nearby students)?
13. Which students receive the most praise and which receive the most criticism? Which students seem to be ignored?
14. Try to determine the extent of any division of labor in the class or within the groups. Are there different roles? Do all carry out the same tasks? Are roles and tasks fixed, or do they shift among students? Who seems to assign these roles or tasks? How smooth running and cohesive is the class and each group?
15. If there are groups, how much communication and sharing exist among them?
16. Is the relationship among the students mostly cooperative, competitive, or individualistic? For example, when the teacher asks a student a question, do other students help the first student answer it, or do they try to answer it themselves?
17. On which students does the teacher rely to help decide when to move on? When teachers decide to move on to another activity or topic, they commonly base this decision on their judgment that certain students have "gotten" the material. This group of students has been termed the "steering group."[2] Where do these students stand in relation to the rest of the class in terms of ability?

Summarize your observations of the students in the classroom. What are the prominent groups and how do the groups interact? Which individuals play key roles in relationships among students and in terms of the lesson flow?

▶

Are students that belong to a minority group treated differently than others? Do any of these students appear to participate in the classroom to a greater or lesser degree? Are there certain kinds of activities in which minority students are more or less engaged?

▶

Students at Risk

Here the focus is on the students we commonly refer to as being "at risk." These are students with a wide range of difficulties, difficulties for which public schools frequently are challenged to provide solutions. The exciting thing about at-risk youths is that, under normal circumstances, they are no less bright or gifted than "low-risk" students. With the right combination of specialized personnel and programming, at-risk students can succeed academically and personally.

Admittedly, *at risk* is a broad term, one that is frequently used without an adequate definition. By *at risk*, I mean quite simply any youth who is apt to chronically make bad choices for himself or herself. The outcomes of these bad decisions are numerous and complex, but they frequently include not graduating from school, drug abuse, heavy drinking, unprotected sex, consistently poor performance in school, and criminal activity. These same youths are also less likely to be active and involved in school activities, communities, houses of worship, and extracurricular clubs (e.g., Scouts, 4-H). Researchers in the field of youth development today seem comfortable describing an individual's overall level of risk in terms of a balance between "risk" and "protective" factors. *Risk factors* are those things that put you in harm's way, such as drug abuse, dropping out of school, and early pregnancy. *Protective factors* are things that counteract or prevent people from making bad choices, such as having a positive and supportive family, being involved in school plays or sports teams, or having a strong connection to the community. When you look at a person's overall risk and protective factors, reason and research support the notion that the more protective factors one has, the more likely one is to develop into a happy, healthy, and productive individual. Conversely, the more risk factors one has, the more likely one is to be in danger of hurting oneself or others and the less likely he or she is to become a positive and productive member of society.[3]

As an observer in a school, you will need to be careful not to cast your judgments in stone. You are thoughtfully observing the behaviors of young people to gain a better understanding of how they interact with each other and how they relate to teachers and to education in general. You are doing this so that you will be better able to connect with a young person and to gain a clearer picture about what this individual needs or doesn't need to help make his or her life easier. The information you collect, combined with your experience, insight, and care, can aid you, a skilled and thoughtful educator, in devising clever ways to energize the nontraditional mind of an at-risk youth.

In Exercise 10.2, you were asked to observe students within their peer groups interacting in the cafeteria or on the playground. In Exercise 10.3, you were asked to observe them interacting with classmates and teachers in the classroom. Did you notice any students who seemed to be acting out in overtly negative ways, who were disengaged completely from what other students were doing, or who were acting in ways that simply made you feel that something was amiss with this student or these students? In just about every school, there are students who don't fit into the regular program, who have nontraditional ways of communicating, who don't excel in subjects taught in schools, and who don't gravitate to or feel comfortable participating in school-sponsored programs.

As you make these observations, remember that many times, you will be incorrect. Someone you thought was at risk might in fact be a model student and vice versa. Also remember that *at risk* is not a synonym for race or socioeconomic status;[4] risk does not discriminate; children and adults, regardless of race, ethnic background, and socioeconomic status, can be in trouble. In most cases, the signs of trouble are evident, but in a few cases, they are not. The best one can do is be open, alert, sensitive, and in contact both with one's own thoughts and emotions and with young people. An individual's risk level can change from year to year and even week to week. With the sustained help of caring and concerned volunteer teachers like you, young people can move from a higher to a lower level of risk.

EXERCISE 10.4

At-Risk Behavior

You may at one time have been involved in activities that would be or have been considered at risk. Yet today you probably stand as a model of success. If this is true, then you are living proof that being at risk doesn't have to mean being out of hope. For this exercise, write a little bit about your at-risk behavior (you can keep this private) and then describe the people or experiences you encountered that caused you to rethink your risky actions.

▶

How did you change your mind and decide not to let these risky actions or behaviors consume you?

▶

Were there other people who helped you?
What was it about these people that made you listen to them?

▶

Have you seen other people make the same mistakes that you have made? How did that make you feel?

▶

If you yourself have never done anything that would be considered risky, then you can talk about a family member, a friend, or a character in a book or a movie that you can remember.

Diversity in the Classroom

With the increasing diversity in U.S. schools, it is more important than ever to take into consideration the instructional needs of individual learners. Students from different social, economic, and cultural backgrounds, not surprisingly, learn best when teachers use strategies compatible with those backgrounds. Here are just a few highlights from some notable studies which demonstrate that students from different backgrounds learn best under specially tailored learning environments. As a teacher, knowing this information can help you immensely as you decide how best to present your lessons.

For many students, the relationships with their teachers can determine to a great extent how much they will learn. Janice Hale found that, because many black students are accustomed to frequent personal interactions at home, they learn best when there is consistent interaction between the teacher and the students.[5] Imani Perry, for example, talks about the closeness between children and adults in black and Hispanic cultures. The adults and children of these families frequently attended the same weekend parties. Through these types of connections, the adults earned children's respect.[6] At school, if black and Hispanic children do not have close relationships with their teachers, the children sometimes do not see a reason to follow their directions or respect their authority.

Roland Tharp and Ronald Gallimore found that native Hawaiian children learned best in classrooms that were structured so that they could work collaboratively with one another.[7] The researchers attributed this phenomenon to social interactions between children and adults in their homes. They found that Hawaiian children took a great deal of responsibility in managing their own daily activities, and that, if not given the same opportunity to do so at school, they would not feel fully engaged.

For women, too, relationships with teachers are important to learning. Mary Belenky found that for a woman's intellectual growth, acceptance and encouragement were most important. The women she interviewed told her that they learned best when they felt secure enough to ask questions, to reveal gaps in their knowledge, and to take risks. Teachers who were perceived to be nonthreatening and who portrayed humans as imperfect and constantly growing better enabled women to feel secure, thus enhancing the learning process.[8]

The physical arrangements of our schools can facilitate learning for students who might otherwise fail. In her article on teaching elementary school Navajo children, Vera John-Steiner describes two contrasting schools and the effects they have on children. She found that one school elicited feelings of "trepidation and fear" in parents and children.[9] A major source of these feelings was the shape of the school building and the arrangement of the desks in the classroom (tall buildings with classrooms where desks were arranged neatly in rows). In another Navajo school, with a very different shape and a more informal classroom structure (the school building was a tent, with students all working around the same table), the children acted very differently. In the second school, the physical setting was more familiar to the students and their families, and the Navajo children under the latter condition who were once described as "shy, were now alert and vocal."[10]

In the modern classrooms of today, issues of diversity are increasingly topics of discussion for educators, administrators, and parents. The notion of diversity in the classroom goes beyond integrating and meeting the needs of students from different sexes, or from different ethnic, racial, social, and economic backgrounds. Consider now what you would do as a teacher if you had children in your classes with speech disorders, visual impairments, Down syndrome, or other analogous conditions. Eva Horn and her colleagues have suggested eight curriculum modifications and adaptations that teachers can make to existing lessons to facilitate the needs of students with disabilities. These modifications range from incorporating specially designed teaching equipment, to modifying the curriculum, to meeting the individual child's cognitive or motor abilities.[11] With many school systems now mandated to integrate children of all abilities into one classroom, you may as a teacher have to consider these points in addition to everything else beginning teachers need to master.

The issue for a teacher or for a student teacher becomes the extent to which your curriculum takes into account students' backgrounds and abilities. Clearly, it is important to examine the extent to which the curriculum, the teacher, and the physical environment impact students. However, no school curriculum can address all the needs of every student. Some teachers, however, provide learning environments that allow different perspectives in the classroom. Whether they help minority students adjust to current school situations or allow students to question society's social and economic foundations, teachers who demonstrate an understanding of and appreciation for the diversity of learning styles in the classroom send a strong message that is supportive of diversity. This message is heard by students, parents, and by the community: Diversity and respect for students' backgrounds and abilities are important not only for the a student's mental health, but also for leveling the playing field for all students as they push forward to achieve their dreams.

NOTES

1. Rob Walker and Clem Adelman, *A Guide to Classroom Observation* (London: Methuen, 1975).
2. Urban Dahllof, *Ability Grouping, Content Validity and Curriculum Process Analysis* (New York: Teacher's College Press, 1971).
3. Peter C. Scales et al., "Contribution of Developmental Assets to the Prediction of Thriving among Adolescents." *Applied Developmental Science,* **4**(1) (2000), 27–46.
4. Robert Kronick, "At Risk Youth: The State of the Art," in *At Risk Youth: Theory Practice, Reform,* ed. Robert Kronick (New York: Garland Publishing, 1997).
5. Janice Hale, *Black Children: Their Roots, Culture, and Learning Styles* (Provo, UT: Brigham Young Press, 1982).
6. Imani Perry, "A Black Student's Reflection on Private and Public Schools." *Harvard Educational Review,* **58** (1988), 332–336.
7. Lily W. Fillmore and Lois M. Meyer, "The Curriculum and Linguistic Minorities," in *Handbook on Research on Curriculum,* ed. Philip Jackson (New York: Macmillan, 1992).
8. Mary Belenky, et al., *A Woman's Way of Knowing: The Development of Self, Voice and Mind* (New York: Basic Books, 1986).
9. Vera John-Steiner et al., eds., *Styles of Learning; Styles of Teaching. The Function of Language in the Classroom* (New York: Teacher's College Press, 1972).
10. Ibid.
11. Eva Horn, J. Lieber et al., eds., *Classroom Models of Individualized Instruction. Widening the Circle: Including Children with Disabilities in Preschool Programs* (New York: Teacher's College Press, 2002).

CHAPTER 11

The Cooperating Teacher

Probably the greatest influence on the quality of a field experience, particularly for a student teacher, is the cooperating teacher. In a sense, the student teacher is an apprentice, and the cooperating teacher is a master teacher. Even in many less formal arrangements, such as exploratory field experiences, there is a cooperating teacher on whom the success of the field experience depends. A cooperating teacher is bound to do some things that a student teacher disagrees with or does not understand. The purpose of this chapter is not to persuade you that the cooperating teacher knows best. Instead, it is meant to help you understand how the cooperating teacher views teaching and to see the situation through his or her eyes.

EXERCISE **11.1**

Conversation with the Teacher

If you can arrange one, a get-acquainted meeting with the cooperating teacher could prove informative.

One purpose of a conversation with the cooperating teacher is to find out the teacher's perspective on teaching and the beliefs underlying the teacher's actions. In order to meet this purpose, objectivity and suspension of judgment are important, even if you strongly disagree with what you hear.

There are many questions you might ask the cooperating teacher. I have organized a series of questions into a set of eight issues. Rather than try to cover all eight in the limited time you can reasonably expect the cooperating teacher to give you, you could select the two or three that interest you most. Your interests may derive from the amount of thought you have personally given to the issues or from the apparent significance of the issues to the co-operating teacher, based on your classroom observations.

The eight issues are as follows (numbers in parentheses refer to the questions in the list following this one):

1. Control
   a. How are decisions made about teaching methods? (1, 2, 3, 5, 6, 9, 11)
   b. How are decisions made about curriculum and content? (4, 5, 9, 10, 11)
   c. How much and what kind of control should teachers have over pupils' behavior? (7, 8, 18)
2. Diversity
   a. What learner differences are significant, and should different types of learners be treated differently? (12)

(continued)

3. Learning
   a. Is learning facilitated by a competitive or cooperative environment? (14)
   b. What is the basis of motivation? (14)
4. Teacher's role
   a. How formal a role should the teacher assume? (13)
5. School and society
   a. How active should a teacher become in political reform? (15)
   b. Should the school reflect the current society or attempt to reform it? (15)
6. Knowledge
   a. What should be the curriculum's emphasis? (16, 18)
   b. Should subject matters be kept separate or integrated? (17)
7. Rewards and criteria
   a. What are the rewards of teaching? (19)
   b. What are the criteria by which teachers should be evaluated? (20, 21)
8. Cooperating teacher–student teacher relationship
   a. What should be the role of the student teacher? (22, 23)

Try to select a time when the cooperating teacher is alone in the classroom or somewhere outside when distractions are minimal. Here are some suggestions for questions covering the eight issues. You will probably have to modify them in your own meeting. Some of the questions might best be left until a future meeting, after you have established a better relationship with the cooperating teacher.

1. I've noticed some special areas in your room. (Specify one of them.) What do you and the kids do in this area? Who gets to use it? How are they selected? (Repeat for each area.)
2. Did you arrange the room this way? (If no:) Who did? (If yes:) What were you trying to do with this arrangement? How long has it been this way?
3. Did you put up the posters, pictures, exhibits, etc., on the walls and bulletin boards? (If no:) Who did? (If yes:) What was the purpose? When did you put them up? (May be different for each poster.)
4. I've been looking through the textbook. How was it selected and by whom? How do you like it? What are its strengths? Weaknesses? Is it successful with some kids but not with others? (Repeat this set of questions for each text.)
5. I also looked over the worksheets, labs, and/or quizzes you've been using. Did you write them? (If no:) Where did you get them? (If yes:) When did you make them up? Did you base them on anything in particular? Are you happy with them?
6. I enjoyed the lesson(s) (or classes) that I had the opportunity to observe. When I compared your lesson plan with the actual lesson, I noticed that you did not follow your plan precisely. (This question is used only if you noticed some discrepancies.) What caused you to modify your plan?
7. What rules do you expect the kids in your class to follow? (*Probe:* rules for waiting their turn to speak and to receive help, rules for moving around the classroom, leaving the classroom, being on time, what to do when finished with work, working together, resolving conflicts among kids, homework, forms to follow, procedures for work, language, noises, who may speak, etc.) Does the school have rules or regulations with which you disagree? (If yes:) Why do you disagree? Do you follow them anyway? Which rules are the most important to you? How do you handle infractions? Are there some kids who break rules more than other kids? Tell me about those kids.
8. How do you enforce your rules? What happens when someone breaks one? Does it depend on who that student is? Do you ever feel you are losing control of the class? How do you go about regaining control?
9. Do parents ever visit the classroom? (If no:) Would you like them to? (If yes:) Are you pleased that they do? How can parents be of most help to you as a teacher? How can they hinder you? Should parents be involved in selection of school books? What about in hiring teachers?

10. Does the school or the district have a curriculum? Are you expected to follow it? Do you? Did you have any say in it? Do you ever depart from it?

11. Do your students' (or "children's," for primary grades) interests affect your teaching methods? (If yes:) In what ways? Do their interests affect the content? Do they have any say in what they study?

12. What sorts of students do you teach? Are there different groups? Could you describe the groups? Do you devote more time to certain students? Do you expect all of them to assume the same degree of responsibility for their learning? Do you use different criteria to evaluate different students? Do you find the diversity among them to be a major problem?

13. How friendly are you with the children? Do you tell them much about yourself? What do you think is the proper role for a teacher?

14. Do you try to develop a sense of competition in your class? How important is cooperating among the kids? What do you use to motivate the kids? (*Probe:* grades, interest and curiosity, comparison of one child's work with another's, fear.)

15. Do you ever let the kids know your political views? Do you think that the schools are doing a pretty good job or do they need to change drastically? Are you trying to help kids fit into the society as it is, or would you like to equip them to reform society?

16. How important are the three Rs to you? What about the children's emotional needs—are they important? What about things like problem-solving skills and creativity—are they important? What is the relative importance of these various goals?

17. Do you ever try to relate one subject matter (e.g., science) with another that you or another teacher teaches? Or do you think different subject matters should be treated separately?

18. What do you test for? How important are your tests and quizzes?

19. Most people have days in their work when they go home feeling especially good because the day and its activities were particularly rewarding. What makes a good day in teaching for you?

20. How do you tell how well you are doing as a teacher? That is, what things provide you with evidence that you're doing a good job?

21. Suppose you accidentally happened to overhear a group of your former students discussing you as a teacher. What kinds of things would you like to hear them saying?

22. Why did you ask to have a student teacher (or aide, depending on your role)?

23. What do you expect from me?

On Form 11.1, summarize the cooperating teacher's responses in column 3 for each issue (expressed as a general question in column 1). The numbers of the question sets that correspond to the issue are listed in column 2.

FORM 11.1 Teacher Analysis Form

(1)	(2)	(3)
Issue	**Question Set Number**	
1. *Control* a. How are decisions made about teaching?	1. Special areas 2. Room arrangement 3. Posters, pictures, etc. 5. Worksheets/labs/quizzes 6. Modification of lesson plan 9. Parents visiting classrooms 11. Student interest affecting teaching methods	

(continued)

EXERCISE **11.1** Continued

Issue	Question Set Number
b. How are decisions made about curriculum and content?	4. Textbook(s) 5. Worksheets/labs/quizzes 9. Parents visiting classrooms 10. School curriculum 11. Student interest affecting teaching methods
c. How much and what kind of control should teachers have over pupils' behavior?	7. Rules/regulations 8. Enforcement of rules 18. Tests
2. *Diversity* a. What pupil differences are significant and should different pupils be treated differently?	12. Groups of children and their treatment
3. *Learning* a. Is learning facilitated by a competitive or cooperative environment?	14. Competition/cooperation/ motivation of students
b. What is the basis for motivation?	14. Competition/cooperation/ motivation of students
4. *Teacher's role* a. How formal a role should the teacher assume in the classroom?	13. Teacher's personal relationship with students
5. *School and society* a. How active should the teacher become in political reform?	15. Political views and reform
b. Should the school reflect the current society or attempt to reform it?	15. Political views and reform
6. *Knowledge* a. What should be the curriculum's emphasis?	16. Three Rs, emotional needs, etc. 18. Areas tested
b. Should subject matters be kept separate or integrated?	17. Separate subject matters
7. *Rewards and criteria* a. What are the rewards of teaching?	19. Good days
b. What are the criteria by which teachers should be evaluated?	20. Doing a good job 21. Overhearing students
8. *Cooperating teacher–student teacher relationship* a. What should be the role of the student teacher?	22. Reason for having a student teacher 23. Expectations

This information about your cooperating teacher is useful for two principal reasons: It prepares you for work within this teacher's classroom and with this teacher's students, and it helps you decide the kind of relationship you may want to develop with this teacher.

First, because the cooperating teacher sets the scene for your field experience, the more you know about the cooperating teacher's perspective on teaching, the more you will understand the context of your own teaching. The cooperating teacher develops in students a set of expectations for "normal" classroom activities and standards of appropriate classroom behaviors and acceptable student performance. These expectations affect how the students will react to any activities in which you try to engage them. For example, if the teacher normally has the students work individually on worksheets at their desks, you might experience some difficulty in having students work cooperatively in small groups on projects.

Second, the degree of comfort you feel with the cooperating teacher's perspective might help you determine the kind of relationship you want to develop with the cooperating teacher. At one extreme, if the cooperating teacher represents all you want to become as a teacher, then you might want to serve in the role of an apprentice for this master teacher. If, on the other extreme, the cooperating teacher represents the opposite of what you wish to become as a teacher, then you might try to establish as much autonomy as possible during the field experience, perhaps working independently with a small group of students on a separate project. Clearly, you are not the only one who determines your role. Cooperating teachers do influence you in several ways during a field experience. They *model* multiple aspects of teaching for you. Many student teachers adopt behaviors simply because they were the only models available to them during this critical period. It is likely that the cooperating teacher has found methods that get results, and so it makes sense to pattern your teaching after them. Cooperating teachers also move student teachers toward conformity; it is often easier to follow the cooperating teacher's lead than change things. Finally, student teachers and aides want to please the cooperating teacher.[1] This might be done out of respect or politeness, but pleasing the cooperating teacher is one way of making a smooth transition into a new situation.

Both the cooperating teacher and your college supervisor contribute to the definition of what is an appropriate role. However, it will be useful at least to understand the situation that your feelings toward the cooperating teacher create for your field experience.

NOTE

1. Derek Anderson, "The Role of Cooperating Teacher's Power in Student Teaching." *Education*, 128(2) (2007), 307–323.

PART FOUR

What Have You Learned?

CHAPTER 12

The Fieldwork Portfolio*

The reflection you have done as part of your field experience has helped you learn about yourself as a teacher and about teaching in general. It has also helped you to explore more deeply the values, assumptions, and beliefs you hold about your learners, the subject matter, and the social context in which your field experience has taken place. This chapter will describe the process by which you may develop a fieldwork portfolio that will allow you to capture some of the important things you've learned through your field experience.

As Wolf describes, "On one level, a schoolteacher's portfolio can be defined as a container for storing and displaying evidence of a teacher's knowledge and skills. However, this definition is incomplete. A portfolio is more than a container—a portfolio also embodies an attitude that . . . the richest portrayals of teacher (and student) are based on multiple sources of evidence collected over time in authentic settings."[1] As an artist may use a portfolio to give others an opportunity to view the development of his or her particular style, so too a teacher may use a portfolio to illustrate how his or her approach to teacher has developed over time.

Here, we will suggest a fieldwork portfolio format that allows you to develop a broad perspective on your field experience by reviewing and rethinking many of the reflective activities you've done thus far. Portfolios are flexible tools that are intended to help illuminate the individuality of each creator. Therefore, they can look quite different from teacher to teacher; they may also be used for different purposes. Portfolios are often used as a means to demonstrate achievements to prospective employers, as an assessment tool that administrators may review, or as a memory aid to help document thoughts about how lessons went and what might be effective to change in future lessons.[2] You or your college supervisor may prefer a format or a purpose for your portfolio different from the one suggested here. If that is the case, you should follow a format or process that best suits your situation.

The Anatomy of a Fieldwork Portfolio

Developing a teaching portfolio is like putting together pieces of a puzzle that when fully assembled present a whole picture. The portfolio, then, is intended to present the picture of who you are as a teacher at this moment. Although it may sometimes feel as

---

*Written with Laurie Vasily.

though your field experience has raised more questions than it has answered, you have learned a tremendous amount through this teaching experience. Developing your own fieldwork portfolio will "make it possible to document the unfolding of both teaching and learning over time."[3]

To determine which items you might include in your fieldwork portfolio, reach back through your reflective papers and try to remember key episodes where your beliefs or assumptions were challenged or reinforced either by the situation, by a learner, or by yourself. As you do this, you will likely find that some of your personal beliefs have changed completely, while others have become even more firm in your mind. Perhaps you have posed questions to yourself in some of your logs for which you still haven't found answers. Including these items in your portfolio will allow you to track the progress of your own development as a teacher. As Loughran and Corrigan explain, "Portfolio items are not an attempt to simplify or summarize the complex, interrelated thoughts and actions associated with teaching and learning; rather they are a way of initiating dialogue about the problematic nature of teaching and learning from their creator's perspective."[4]

A concluding reflective paper serves as the centerpiece of the fieldwork portfolio format we recommend here. This paper allows you an opportunity to sit back from the day-to-day activities of your field experience and to draw some conclusions about what you've learned from it as a whole. In addition to the reflective paper, other items included may illustrate issues highlighted in the paper, demonstrate achievement of a goal, or describe the progress of a particular learner. Some of our students have developed fieldwork portfolios that include artwork or poetry, or are placed within elaborately decorated boxes or folders. Other students have felt more comfortable including their written reflections only. The items you choose to include and the wrapper in which you include the items may be determined by the portfolio's purpose, but nevertheless, should allow readers insight into the individuality of its creator. Items that some of our students have included in their portfolios include the following:

- Selected fieldwork logs
- A reflective paper on goals and concerns
- Lesson plans
- Self-analyses of teaching episodes
- A statement of your personal theory of teaching
- Overheads or handouts used in a lesson
- Videotapes of a teaching episode
- Audiotapes of an activity with students
- Fieldwork supervisor's evaluation or recommendation letter
- Feedback from learners
- Materials created with learners

The following are some initial questions that may be helpful to answer as you undertake the task of developing your fieldwork portfolio:

- How would you describe the context of your fieldwork?
- What were the goals and concerns you had at the outset of your fieldwork?
- Have you reached your goals or addressed your concerns? How have they changed?
- What are the issues that stand out for you most in reflecting on your field experience?
- What can you now say about teaching in general?
- What can you now say about yourself as a teacher?

Context

An effective place to begin your fieldwork portfolio is with a brief description of the social and physical contexts in which your field experience took place. Paint a picture for the reader of the teaching situation and your role in it by describing the community, the institution, and the group. Use this section to set the stage for the drama that will unfold. That is, provide enough background information so that a reader completely unfamiliar with your field experience will gain an understanding of its essence. It may be helpful at this point to refer to the situation analysis you wrote earlier (Chapters 8 through 11).

Goals and Concerns

Reflecting on your goals and concerns for your fieldwork (Chapters 2 and 7), think about how you now feel about them. You may find that your goals shifted as you gained familiarity with the context of your field experience. If so, describe how they shifted and why. Most important, describe the extent of progress you feel you've made toward fulfilling your goals and addressing your concerns.

Themes

As you read through your fieldwork logs, look for a central theme that runs through them. For example, some of your logs may have addressed discipline issues; some may have addressed the teacher–learner relationship; maybe they addressed your relationship with your cooperating teacher; or perhaps, your logs seem to focus a lot of attention on one or two particular students. In any case, these themes are issues on which you have focused much reflection over the course of your fieldwork. For this section, briefly review what you were thinking about the theme as you wrote your logs. You do not have to reiterate fully each episode, simply refer to particular logs that help to illuminate the theme (and include those particular logs in the portfolio). Compare that thinking with how you now think about the theme. In this way, you can chart the course of the development of your professional knowledge around that particular theme.

Personal Theory of Teaching

As you explored in Chapter 7, your personal perspective and beliefs about teaching influence who you are as a teacher. Who you are as a teacher, in turn, affects what you do in the classroom. As Clark and Peterson note, "A teacher's cognitive and other behaviors are guided by and make sense in relation to a personally held system of beliefs, values and principles."[5]

Through the reflective activities you have undertaken as part of your fieldwork, you have made more explicit your own beliefs, values, and principles. People refer to their own systems of personal beliefs, values, and principles in different ways: as a philosophy of teaching, an approach to teaching, a teaching perspective, or a personal theory of teaching. Here, we use the phrase "personal theory of teaching," because we believe it captures the essence of an evolving thought process inherent in reflective teaching.

Your personal theory of teaching statement should paint a concise picture (in one or two pages) of your beliefs about teaching. The following questions may help guide your thinking about your personal theory of teaching:

- What is the ultimate goal of education? Why should people be educated?
- What do you believe is the role of the teacher?
- What do you believe about learners? Are they all capable of the same thing? Why or why not?

Although it may seem a difficult task to capture all the elements of your own personal theory of teaching, there are some tools that can help. Dennis Fox describes how metaphors can be used to illustrate personal theories of teaching.[6] He categorizes theories into four different basic categories:

- *Transfer theories* view learners as empty vessels into which a teacher may pour knowledge or information. If you espouse this view, you may think of the teaching endeavor as being similar to water being poured into a pitcher. Or you may think of a teacher as being similar to a baby food manufacturer who must break down the subject matter to make it "digestible" for less-developed minds.
- *Shaping theories* view learners as malleable substances that can be molded into a form determined by the teacher. Some metaphors that describe this view are the teacher as a metal worker or an artist, who forms the raw material into a certain finished product.
- As the name suggests, *traveling theories* view education as a journey and the teacher as a guide or leader. Learners may have some say in determining the direction of the journey, and teaching can be thought of as a process of climbing a number of small hills, or surmounting a very large mountain. In either case, the teacher is considered akin to either a local guide who may have already fully explored the terrain or as a partner in exploration.
- *Growing theories* view teaching and learning as a process of nurturing development. In this view, learning can be thought of in terms of gardening using fertile soil. The teacher, as the gardener, "may have broad plans as to how he wants the garden to develop (probably rather flexible ones, which change as possibilities within the garden reveal themselves), but he does not attempt to specify the exact dimensions that each plant (or concept structure) is to achieve."[7]

These categories of theories may help you think through a metaphor that illustrates what you believe about teaching. Or you may have a metaphor in mind that better describes your own personal theory of teaching. As you think about the elements of the metaphor, keep in mind that metaphors are necessarily limited and may not fully capture every aspect of your theory. If you use a metaphor in stating your personal theory of teaching, take time to reflect on the limitations of the metaphor. Include a discussion of these limitations in your statement, so it is clear to the reader that your theory isn't just a simple picture but a joining together of your personal values, beliefs, and principles.

Developing your fieldwork portfolio allows you the opportunity to look back on your field experience and the reflective writing you're doing about it. As such, it is a tool through which you are able to develop professionally as a teacher. As Richert mentions,

> The ability to think about what one does and why—assessing past actions, current situations, and intended outcomes—is vital to intelligent practice, practice that is reflective and not routine. As the time in the teaching process when teachers stop to think about their work and make sense of it, reflection influences how one grows as a professional by influencing how successfully one is able to learn from one's experiences.[8]

Epilogue

When I was a student in school, I could not understand why people called the endpoint of schooling *commencement*. It was so confusing to me that I found myself using the word *commence* to mean *terminate*. Of course, *commencement* refers to the beginning of life after school. What I realized much later is that we can consider the conclusion of any experience as a commencement, a period of getting ready for the next experience.

This book has focused on preparing for and reflecting on one particular experience. The conclusion of one particular experience is an opportune time for both reflection and preparation. It is a time to think back over one teaching experience and attempt to use it as a basis for planning the next experience.

Now might be a good time to make some plans for the future. While your field experience is still fresh in your mind, consider the following questions:

1. a. What issues have been raised by your field experience? Which ones remain unresolved?

    ▶

    b. What sorts of experiences do you think will enable you to work out some of these issues?

    ▶

2. a. What teaching skills do you need to work on?

    ▶

    b. How might you work on them?

    ▶

3. What kinds of teaching situations do you now need to try?

    ▶

4. What should you be doing in the meantime (e.g., types of books to read, people to talk with, observations to make)?

    ▶

NOTES

1. Kenneth Wolf, "The Schoolteacher's Portfolio: Issues in Design, Implementation, and Evaluation." *Phi Delta Kappan*, 73 (1991), 129–136.
2. Hilda Borko, Paul Michalec, Maria Timmons, and James Siddle, "Student Teaching Portfolios: A Tool for Promoting Reflective Practice." *Journal of Teacher Education*, 48(5) (1997), 345–357.
3. Wolf, "The Schoolteacher's Portfolio."
4. John Loughran and Deborah Corrigan, "Teaching Portfolios: A Strategy for Developing Learning and Teaching in Preservice Education." *Teaching and Teacher Education*, 11(6) (1995), 565–577.
5. Christopher M. Clark and Penelope L. Peterson, "Teachers' Thought Processes," in *Handbook of Research on Teaching*, ed. Merlin. C. Wittrock (New York: Macmillan, 1985), pp. 255–296.
6. Dennis Fox, "Personal Theories of Teaching." *Studies in Higher Education*, 8(2) (1983), 151–163.
7. Andy Northedge, "Examining Our Implicit Analogies for Learning Processes," *Programmed Learning and Educational Technology*, 4(13) (1976), 67–78.
8. Anna E. Richert, "Teaching Teachers to Reflect: A Consideration of Programme Structure." *Journal of Curriculum Studies*, 22(6) (1990), 509–527.

Appendixes

APPENDIX

A Instruments

The Student Belief Inventory

Many of the beliefs we, as teachers, hold are derived from our perspectives as students. Later in this appendix, you will respond to a set of statements designed to help you identify your perspective on your field experience as a teacher. In this exercise, you will respond to a set of statements intended to elicit your perspective on being a student.

Note: 1 = Strongly disagree ("For the most part, no")
2 = Disagree but with major qualifications ("No, but . . .")
3 = Agree but with major qualifications ("Yes, but . . .")
4 = Strongly agree ("For the most part, yes")

Control

1. My instructors should have complete control over each of the following:
1 2 3 4   **a.** teaching methods
1 2 3 4   **b.** classroom rules
1 2 3 4   **c.** selection of textbooks
1 2 3 4   **d.** curriculum and goals
1 2 3 4   **e.** administration of the school

2. Each of the following individuals or groups should have a say in educational decisions that affect each of my classes:
1 2 3 4   **a.** college administrators
1 2 3 4   **b.** the faculty member in charge
1 2 3 4   **c.** other faculty members
1 2 3 4   **d.** myself
1 2 3 4   **e.** my parents
1 2 3 4   **f.** state officials
1 2 3 4   **g.** students in each class

3. Each of the following individuals or groups should have a say in the courses I take:
1 2 3 4   **a.** faculty members
1 2 3 4   **b.** state officials
1 2 3 4   **c.** my parents
1 2 3 4   **d.** myself
1 2 3 4   **e.** college administrators

Diversity

4. As a student, I want to be treated like all other students when it comes to each of the following:

1 2 3 4   **a.** methods
1 2 3 4   **b.** evaluation criteria
1 2 3 4   **c.** time offered to students
1 2 3 4   **d.** teachers' expectations for my achievement level

Learning

1 2 3 4   **5.** I learn best when lessons are laid out as a series of carefully sequenced steps.
1 2 3 4   **6.** I learn best when left on my own to figure things out.
1 2 3 4   **7.** My motivation for learning derives more from intrinsic interest and curiosity than from external rewards.

Role of the Teacher

1 2 3 4   **8.** It is more important for me to respect than to like my instructors.
1 2 3 4   **9.** I prefer my instructors to be friendly and personal rather than to project a businesslike attitude.

School and Society

1 2 3 4   **10.** I don't think it proper for my instructors to let students know about their political preferences or their criticisms of the college administration.
1 2 3 4   **11.** Everything that I learn is related to every other thing.
1 2 3 4   **12.** All students (including myself) should have to study a core of studies that represent the basic elements of a good education.
1 2 3 4   **13.** My education should emphasize a broad background in the liberal arts, rather than specialized training.

It might be interesting to compare your responses on the Student Belief Inventory with those of your classmates. How do you account for differences and similarities? Another interesting comparison is your responses to the Student Belief Inventory versus your responses to the Teacher Belief Inventory that follows. While responding to the statements in the Teacher Belief Inventory, you will be able to reflect on the degree to which your perspective on teaching has been influenced by your student perspective and the appropriateness of one to the other.

The Teacher Belief Inventory*

What if in your field experience you were fully responsible for the learners? Would you be the same teacher as the cooperating teacher or your co-worker(s) (if any), or would you differ in significant ways?

This exercise is designed to help you sort out your beliefs. In order to do it, you must decide the extent to which you, as the teacher in charge, agree or disagree with

*This inventory was adapted from an instrument developed by Ken Zeichner and Bob Tabachnick at the University of Wisconsin—Madison.

each of the following assertions. If you are not actually the teacher in charge in your field experience, respond *as if you were in charge*. Circle one response for each assertion. Respond only to those assertions that apply to your field experience. You will note that the assertions are grouped under headings corresponding to the six basic issues presented in Chapter 5.

> Note: 1 = Strongly disagree ("For the most part, no")
> 2 = Disagree but with major qualifications ("No, but . . .")
> 3 = Agree but with major qualifications ("Yes, but . . .")
> 4 = Strongly agree ("For the most part, yes")

Control

1 2 3 4   **1.** I would encourage parents to work with me inside the classroom.

1 2 3 4   **2.** Parents would have no right to tell me as a teacher what to do in the classroom.

1 2 3 4   **3.** As a teacher, I should be left free to determine the methods of instruction that I use in the classrooms.

1 2 3 4   **4.** Parents would have the right to visit my classroom at any time if they gave me prior notice.

1 2 3 4   **5.** I would consider the revision of my teaching methods if these were criticized by the learners.

1 2 3 4   **6.** As a teacher, I would rely heavily on the textbook and prepackaged materials rather than try to write and design my own.

1 2 3 4   **7.** Learners should have some control over the order in which they complete classroom assignments.

1 2 3 4   **8.** Learners should have some choice in the selection of classroom assignments.

1 2 3 4   **9.** I would feel free to depart from the official adopted curriculum when it seemed appropriate to do so.

1 2 3 4 **10.** Parents and other community members should have the right to reject school books and materials.

1 2 3 4 **11.** The principal or my department chairperson should ultimately determine what and how I should teach.

1 2 3 4 **12.** What I teach will probably be heavily influenced by state-wide or district-wide standardized tests.

1 2 3 4 **13.** As a teacher, my primary task would be to carry out the educational goals and curricular decisions that have been formulated by others.

1 2 3 4 **14.** I would give learners some options for deciding *what* to study.

1 2 3 4 **15.** Parents should be active in formulating the curriculum.

1 2 3 4 **16.** Parents should be involved in hiring teachers for their children's school.

1 2 3 4 **17.** I would be involved in administrative decisions in my school or organization (e.g., allocating the school's budget, hiring staff).

1 2 3 4 **18.** I would disobey official regulations when I felt that they interfered with the welfare of the learners.

1 2 3 4 **19.** I would allow learners to go to the bathroom at just about any time.

1 2 3 4 **20.** It is more important for learners to learn to obey rules than to make their own decisions.

1 2 3 4 **21.** I would encourage learners to speak spontaneously without necessarily raising their hands.

Diversity

1 2 3 4   **22.** I would employ multiple and diverse criteria to evaluate learners. It is not fair to use the same criteria to evaluate all learners.

1 2 3 4   **23.** If I taught classes that differed with regard to learners' academic ability, I would teach them differently.

1 2 3 4   **24.** I would not expect learners from economically disadvantaged backgrounds to assume the same degree of responsibility for their learning as learners from more economically advantaged backgrounds.

1 2 3 4   **25.** One of the main problems in classrooms today is diversity among pupils.

1 2 3 4   **26.** There should be set standards for each grade level and subject, and as a teacher I would evaluate all learners according to these standards.

1 2 3 4   **27.** I could probably do most for learners who want to learn.

1 2 3 4   **28.** I would attempt to devote more of my time to the least capable learners in order to provide an equal education for all.

1 2 3 4   **29.** I would lower my expectations regarding academic performance for those learners who come from economically disadvantaged backgrounds.

Learning

1 2 3 4   **30.** One of the most important tasks I would face as a teacher is developing individuals into a good working group.

1 2 3 4   **31.** I would use the comparison of one learner's work with that of another as a method of motivation.

1 2 3 4   **32.** People learn better when cooperating than when competing with one another.

1 2 3 4   **33.** I would lead learners through a series of easily mastered steps in such a way that the learners make as few errors as possible.

1 2 3 4   **34.** I would tell my students exactly what was expected of them in terms of behavior, homework, and lesson objectives.

1 2 3 4   **35.** Because people learn a great deal from their mistakes, I would allow learners to learn by trial and error.

1 2 3 4   **36.** I would use grades to motivate learning.

1 2 3 4   **37.** The sheer interest in learning something new and challenging or of successfully accomplishing a task usually supplies sufficient motivation for learning.

Teacher's Role

1 2 3 4   **38.** I would start out as a strict disciplinarian and gradually become more approachable as the learners come to respect my authority.

1 2 3 4   **39.** As a teacher, I would tell learners a great deal about myself.

1 2 3 4   **40.** I would serve more as a group facilitator than as a transmitter of information.

School and Society

1 2 3 4   **41.** My political beliefs have no place in my teaching.

1 2 3 4   **42.** Schools and youth groups should seek to help all learners to fit as smoothly as possible into our present society.

1 2 3 4   **43.** I would not participate in local political activities when it involved criticism of local school authorities.

1 2 3 4   **44.** As a teacher, I would be concerned with changing society.

1 2 3 4   **45.** There is a great deal wrong with the public schools today, and one of my priorities as a teacher would be to contribute as much as possible to the reform of public schooling.

1 2 3 4   **46.** The home backgrounds of many learners are the major reasons that those children do not succeed in school.

1 2 3 4   **47.** Schooling as it now exists helps perpetuate social and economic inequalities in our society.

Knowledge

1 2 3 4   **48.** It is as important for learners to enjoy learning as it is for them to acquire specific skills.

1 2 3 4   **49.** In the elementary grades, instruction in the three Rs should take up most of the school day. Other subject areas (e.g., science, social studies) should be given less emphasis in the curriculum.

1 2 3 4   **50.** Students in high school don't spend enough time on the "basic" subjects.

1 2 3 4   **51.** Most high school courses try to cover too much material, thereby sacrificing real understanding.

1 2 3 4   **52.** My subject matter is more a body of content than it is a set of skills to be mastered.

1 2 3 4   **53.** One of the primary purposes of teaching my subject matter is to develop good work and study habits.

1 2 3 4   **54.** Schools today pay too much attention to the social–emotional needs of children, and not enough emphasis is given to academic skill development.

1 2 3 4   **55.** I would emphasize teaching the three Rs more than the skills of problem solving.

1 2 3 4   **56.** It would be important to me to divide the school day into clearly designated times for different subject areas.

1 2 3 4   **57.** I would teach the knowledge of different subject areas separately, because important knowledge is overlooked when subjects are integrated.

APPENDIX

B Sample Logs and Fieldwork Portfolios

Sample Logs

Log for December 1—Erin Tompkins

Sequence of Events
1. Arrival—end of eighth period
2. Ninth period—helped Sharad study science
3. After-school program—worked on science with Ricki, P. K., and Tom
4. Late bus duty with Ms. Soto
5. Departure

Episode.   I was helping Ricki and P. K. fill out a table about the location and function of the different cell parts. P. K. asked me a question and two other students laughed at him. I began to answer his question when Ms. Soto came over to the table where we were working and yelled at P. K. She said, "P. K. I don't need you distracting other students who are trying to get their work done." He started to tell her what he asked me and she said, "I don't care. You can leave the room if you don't knock it off. Just do your work and be quiet or you're out!" She then apologized to me and went back to helping another student.

Analysis.   I was very frustrated after this episode. This is the first time I've seen Ms. Soto raise her voice with a student and accuse him of causing problems when he was getting his work done and other students were being disruptive. P. K. had asked me a legitimate question; the other students who laughed at him were the problem. I was frustrated because Ricki and P. K. were working hard and asking me good questions. I was annoyed that P. K. was being reprimanded for asking a question that was relevant to the topic we were working on. I also felt helpless because I wanted to tell Ms. Soto that it wasn't P. K. who was the problem. I didn't feel it was my place to correct her in front of her students and kept quiet. I decided that my saying something would only make things worse because it would encourage P. K. to continue arguing with Ms. Soto, and he would be in more trouble.

The most frustrating thing about this episode for me was P. K.'s reaction. He had seemed very interested in actually learning about the cell, and he was asking a lot of questions. After Ms. Soto yelled at him, he didn't ask questions. He just filled in the answers as Ricki found them in the reading. This really bothered me because P. K. and Ricki had been working well together, and after he was reprimanded, P. K. chose to shut down. I don't blame him. I'm sure that it was very difficult for him to be called disruptive when he was working hard and actively participating in the work. He was probably discouraged and angry because Ms. Soto just assumed that he was the problem. I think he decided it would be easier to sit quietly and not participate.

I was unable to observe the effect of this episode on the entire class. My back was to the classroom, but things were quieter for a few minutes, so I assume everyone was surprised and a little confused. Ms. Soto doesn't get angry very often, and it was strange that she chose that moment to get so upset.

Ms. Soto explained to me after class that P. K. is a loud and disruptive student and she didn't want him getting in the way of the other students' learning. She also said that P. K. wasn't a student in her classes during the day, so she didn't care how he was doing and she wasn't going to put up with him being a problem during the after-school program. I think it was unfair of her to assume that P. K. was the problem because she has had problems with him before. It also bothered me that she didn't care how he did because he wasn't her responsibility. He was obviously trying to improve, since he came to the after-school program on his own, and it was unfair of her to treat him that way.

I'm sure P. K. is disruptive at times, but I hope when I'm in a situation like this, I behave differently than Ms. Soto. My guess is she'd had a bad day and needed to vent her anger. Unfortunately, she chose to take it out on P. K. because she'd had problems with him before. Her choice caused a student to shut down for the rest of the time he was there. If I were dealing with this situation, I would have waited to see what was happening before I said anything to anybody. Waiting to say something would give me more time to assess the situation and be sure that I was speaking to the student who needed it. Without taking time to think it would be easy simply to take my frustrations out on a student I didn't like as much as the others in the class.

Sample Log—High School

Log for March 27—Kelli Dwyer
Westville High School

Sequence of Events
1. Arrived at Westville High School
2. Seventh-period pre-algebra begins
3. I work with small group—Sally, Mark, Maya, and Lee
4. Maya gets upset—change plans
5. Get back to finish lesson

Episode. I arrived at 1:45 and went straight to Ms. Carver's room. My four students were already in the conference room waiting for me. I wondered what was going on since they were there 5 minutes early. I went into the classroom and spoke to Ms. Carver. She gave me some problems to go over with the students and told me that Maya was having some family issues and so she had let the four of them go wait for me a few minutes early. I grabbed my textbook and went to the conference room. I walked in and sat down. Everyone said "hi" but Maya kept looking down at the table. I passed around the problems and then got back up and went over to the chalk board to work through some examples. We were adding fractions so I wrote $5/6 + 6/5 = ?$ on the board and asked for volunteers. They were all working on it and Mark raised his hand and said, "11/30" so I asked Maya if she agreed with that answer. She started crying and telling me she didn't feel like doing anything because her Dad was really ill. I told her I was sorry and I asked her if she needed to leave and she said she didn't. Everyone else just sat there quietly. I tried another problem but they couldn't focus because she was still upset, so I asked Maya if we could go outside for a minute and talk. She got up and we went out. I told her that the guidance counselor could talk to her or let her sit in a quiet place. I told her that she needed to talk to someone when she felt this way. I walked her over to the office and told Mrs. St. Ledger that Maya needed to see the counselor. I told her goodbye and went back to the others. Lee was making light of Maya's reaction. I told them Maya was going to stay in the office and we talked a bit about how she must feel and what people could do to help her. Then we worked for the rest of the period.

Analysis.   I learned right away how important flexibility is in the classroom. In order to keep things moving when something unexpected happens. I realized I had to be able to understand the situation, process it quickly, try to work it out, and in this case change and act on a new decision. Originally, I was going to see if she could stay in the class, but when she remained upset, I decided I needed to get her some help, so I stopped the lesson and took care of her. I knew we would not get a lot done since the others were affected by her crying. The normal routine was not going to work but the students learned, I hope, one way to care for others and show compassion. I realized that the lessons learned are not always the ones we plan on. I feel that I handled this much better than I would have last semester. I probably would have panicked and run to get the teacher. Today I didn't tell Ms. Carver until the period was over. I was also able to see that learning was not going to happen at that moment, where I probably would have just plowed ahead before, oblivious to whether they were listening to me or not.

Ms. Carver and I talked after class and she told me that Maya's father has been battling with cancer and can't restart chemo for four more weeks. I told her how I handled the situation and she told me that there are many of those moments in teaching when a student needs to be guided or moved to a different place. When interacting with my students, I try to keep a line between us that, in the end, lets me do a better job of helping them. I know that some of them would like to be friends but it is important for me to remain their teacher.

I needed to have the teacher hat on when I came back in and saw Lee smirking about Maya. I told him and the others that this was a hard time for her and they really needed to respect her and her situation. Lee said he was just goofing around but I told him that it wasn't the best way to act. He mumbled a bit, but I then went straight into the lesson and did not dwell on it or lecture him—I know how much I hate it when people do that to me. After a few minutes, we were back into the math and everyone seemed fine when we finished. I know that it wasn't that long ago I would probably not have said anything for fear that Lee would have thought I was a jerk. But I see the role that I need to take as the teacher.

I still would like to be more adept at handling situations when students need to talk or have a problem. I still felt like I needed to sweep her problem under the rug as quickly as possible since it was making everyone uncomfortable. I've seen Ms. Carver put her arm around a student and talk to him quietly and seem to act like a parental figure. I can't see myself doing that just yet. Overall, a very interesting day.

Log for October 21—Tony Puliafico

Sequence of Events
1. I arrive at Martin Luther King Elementary School.
2. Rachel arrives with her class from their gym section; they sit down and practice handwriting.
3. I help review division with a section of students; I spend most of my time helping one student.
4. Rachel administers a spelling test to her class.
5. Rachel again divides the class; I discuss the concept of division with five students.

Episode.   As the students entered the classroom, I noticed a girl who had never been in class before. She began to practice her handwriting like the others, but she kept talking to Marc, another student. Eventually, I approached Marc and told him to stop talking. He told me, "She doesn't speak English, she's Bosnian. I speak Bosnian too, so I'm helping her." Enlightened by this new knowledge, I allowed them to talk.

Later, Rachel reviewed math. She put me and another teacher's assistant on opposite sides of the classroom. I was on the Bosnian girl's side. I took a seat in front of her desk and listened to Rachel. Stefka, the Bosnian girl, solved several subtraction problems without difficulty. However, when Rachel explained division and assigned some problems, Stefka could not do them. I drew sticks representing numbers and circled certain sets to explain each problem. For example, when she had to divide 24 by 8, I drew 24 sticks and circled groups of 8. Stefka understood and wrote down the answer.

Soon enough, Rachel came to check on Stefka. She watched as I used my stick-drawing method. I explained my plan to Rachel to justify what I was doing. She responded, "Your way's great. She doesn't understand English, so you have to use other ways." She observed for a little while longer before leaving. I helped Stefka in this way as she progressed through the assignment. She was able to do some problems on her own, and I helped her with the more challenging ones. Eventually, Rachel returned with a bucket of plastic chips. Instead of drawing sticks, we started using these chips to explain division. Stefka caught on quickly and began to use the chips herself. Using both stick drawings and these chips, Stefka completed the assignment.

Analysis. I was rather apprehensive when encountering this experience. I had never dealt with a non-English-speaking student before. I knew that words wouldn't help Stefka at all, yet I spoke anyway. But I knew to use universal symbols and gestures. Nonverbal communication saved me last Monday, and hopefully, it helped Stefka to learn.

All in all, I was quite proud of my achievement in the classroom. First, this incident made me feel like a real *teacher*. I wasn't spewing information or making students memorize certain facts. I used my own resources to convey a new concept to Stefka. She forced me to teach. Spewing information wouldn't have helped her at all. I needed to make her understand. Luckily, I was teaching math. I was able to express division without using words. Basically, I represented numbers with sticks. I was worried that Stefka wouldn't understand, but she caught on right away. As soon as I demonstrated one problem to her, she began to use the same format on other problems.

My dilemma with Stefka actually opened my eyes to other situations. The methods I used with Stefka could be used for any student who was having trouble understanding a concept. Sometimes, I lose sight of the fact that there are many ways to teach something. I could just as easily use sticks and circles to explain division to an English-speaking student. When a student doesn't understand a concept, I should more often revert to basics. In this specific case, division is nothing more than breaking down a number into smaller numbers. Just as Stefka understood this basic definition of division, so would any other student. In the future, I hope to remember to "go back to basics" when a child doesn't understand something.

Thinking back, I have to wonder if Stefka really belonged in that class. She couldn't speak a word of English. In fact, she just moved to this country. How can anyone expect her to learn without knowing the language? When I look at the entire situation, though, I realize that she's learning more than any other student in that class. Hundreds of people have told me that the best way to learn a language is to immerse yourself in it. Stefka will begin to pick up English just by hearing it every day. And this is essential—she'll have to learn English if she's going to live here. Also, Stefka can use Marc as an aid in the classroom. From what I observed, Marc explained to her anything she didn't understand. He helped her with the handwriting assignment and acted like a translator for Rachel. Rachel often called on Marc to help Stefka during class. Marc's presence has probably made Stefka's transition much smoother and less intimidating.

Helping Stefka was my first real accomplishment in Rachel's class. On the other days I'd been there, I had just played money games with the students and stood around the classroom. It felt very satisfying actually to teach. I gained a lot of confidence in myself from this experience. I had been worried about what Rachel thought of me, if I helped her or if I might have been hindering her teaching. But she let me know that I was accomplishing a lot by connecting with Stefka. Also, I don't know if the students really consider me a teacher yet. They think they can get away with goofing off around me, and they seem shocked when I reprimand them. They seem to be getting used to me, and they'll learn my role in the classroom. But also, as Rachel trusts me more, I may begin teaching even more, and the students will realize that I am, in fact, there to teach.

For the first time, I felt satisfied walking out of Rachel's classroom last week. I feel that I handled the situation well. I taught a student who really needed extra help and attention. With my confidence and motivation higher, I hope to return to class next week and teach some more.

Log for December 5—Lisa Pinsker

Sequence of Events
1. Arrived at activities center
2. Set up the conference room for the activity
3. Showed "telescopes" to a few children
4. Went to the assembly
5. Facilitated astronomy activity for three more periods
6. Went home

Episode.   On Friday at the activities center, we learned about astronomy through various creative activities. One of these activities was to throw some beads down on a black sheet of paper; the pattern they made on the sheet was to be a constellation. The children had to look at the bead patterns, glue the beads down on the paper, and decide what the pattern looked like to them. Then they could name their constellation and create an accompanying story. At first, few children showed interest in the activity; however, once Jen and I made our own, some students began to take an interest. Jen made a constellation of a turtle; I made one that, to me, looked like a cat chasing a butterfly and named it "Shoshie" (after my first cat). I had the children help me out with it, before I made my final decision on what it was. I even wrote a short story about the cat, Shoshie, and how she and the butterfly became a constellation. One 6-year-old boy, Martin, took a special interest in my constellation and story. He listened to my story, and immediately started making his own constellation. When Martin completed his constellation, he told me it was a snake. He then asked, "Will you write for me?" I said, "Yes." He proceeded to tell me that his constellation was called "Shohe." He then dictated Shohe's story to me; the story followed the exact structure as my story of Shoshie. When I finished writing out his story, I asked Martin to share it with the other students. He told his story, and we then continued with the other activities.

Analysis.   This astronomy activity session was especially fun for me, because astronomy is one of my favorite hobbies. I actually planned these activities, and intended for them to be an outlet for imagination and creativity, rather than a formal lesson in astronomy. The constellation-making activity is one that I enjoyed immensely. I really got into my picture and story. I was eager to help my students do the same.

They say that "Imitation is the sincerest form of flattery." I must admit I was quite surprised when Martin explained his constellation to me. It had an amazing resemblance to mine. I was shocked at how similar his story was to my story, considering I had only told my story to him once. It was indeed flattering that he remembered my story well enough to duplicate it with his snake. When Martin said that he wanted to name his constellation "Shohe," I was confused; it took me a minute to realize that he wanted to name it the same as mine, but wanted to change the gender to a "he." It was a clever manipulation of the letters in the name. I found it almost comical. Still,

I guess I was a bit disappointed that he did not think of the name more independently. I did not say anything to him about it, because I knew he named the constellation what he wanted to name it; I did not want to intrude on his decision.

I have mixed feelings about the whole situation; on the one hand, I feel it was cute and clever for him to adapt his constellation to mine; on the other hand, I wish he had created a more original piece. I wanted him to be creative and imaginative. When I think about it, I suppose he was; his story was very well spoken, eloquent in fact, and his assessment of the picture as a snake was very creative. I do not know; I guess I have always tried to think of my own unique ideas. It is a foreign feeling to me that Martin mimicked my work so closely. It did feel good to see and to know that Martin thought so highly of my constellation. It also made me feel good that Martin was inspired to try it out for himself. Many students did not even attempt this activity; Martin went in motivated and eager to create. I love seeing that kind of eagerness in a child.

Maybe I should have said something to him about the name right from the start. I am still unsure if I handled the situation correctly. I might be making too big a deal of this episode, but, for some reason, the incident stayed with me. I cannot adequately explain how Martin made me feel; the exchange left me ambivalent about my own actions. In retrospect, I think I did the right thing. I let Martin be free to make his own decision and to create on his own, even if the ideas were borrowed. I guess everyone receives inspiration from one source or another. In this case, the inspiration was just a bit more direct than I am used to. Overall, I was quite pleased with the results of the activity; I know I will always keep my Shoshie constellation and think back on how much fun I had and on the efforts of one small boy.

Log for March 30—Sara Kelley
Evenville After-School Camp

Sequence of Events
> 3:00–3:15 PM Welcome students, free reading
> 3:15–3:30 PM Walked to playground
> 3:30–4:00 PM Snack, nature talk
> 4:00–4:45 PM Free play with elementary after-school program
> 4:45–5:00 PM Walked back to camp
> 5:00–5:15 PM Younger kids went home, cleanup

Episode.   Jeff was playing in the sandbox to my right with several other kids while I sat on the bench with SueSan, her head on my leg because she was overheated from running in the sun. Jeff and I were playing a make-believe game involving cars and cakes all made from sand and plastic cups. Very little was said between us during his play. Jeff had a running commentary on what he was doing, and I interjected with an occasional, "neat," "yep," or "how fun" in response to what I half-heard. As time went on he changed gradually from keeping the sand on the ground to lifting it up and pouring it to tossing it in the air and watching the dust fly to finally throwing the sand out of the cup into the direction of other children. The other kids didn't make any comments about the sand that was being thrown near them; they continued to work on a castle that was about half the length of the sandbox. When I saw Jeff throw the sand I don't know if it was the first time or not but I said, "Please don't throw the sand, Jeff, it needs to stay in the box." Without answering he went back to playing but very quickly threw the sand toward the other side of the box again. I looked up because I heard the swish of sand being thrown and said in the voice I reserve for making demands, "Do not throw any more sand, or you will have to leave this area." Jeff made eye contact with me but neither of us changed our neutral expressions. He sat back down and I gave him more of my attention, asking him questions about what he was doing and listening to what he said, responding with more specific statements than I had used earlier. Jeff poured sand from cup to cup while we talked and made up stories. He did not throw sand for the remainder of our time outside.

Analysis.   Jeff and I have spent a large portion of my time at the camp together. When we play or read together, it is usually one-on-one instead of in groups. It is rare for Jeff to be a discipline problem when clear limits are set for him. On my first day at the camp, Jeff continued to misbehave on our walk when I asked him to stop. Since then, he has come to see me in a position of authority, and I believe we have fun together.

I've noticed that his behavior usually follows the same pattern it did in this episode; he does something he probably knows he shouldn't, waits to be told to stop, and does the action again. If a more forceful request is given, he will obey it. This happens especially when another child is consuming my attention as SueSan was because she was sick.

Jeff has the most problems when I make a request and then leave or do something else with another child. When he doesn't see that it's a request I'm going to enforce, he can become disruptive during the activity. Because this is an after-school program, we try to keep the rules to a minimum, and I especially dislike sounding mean and constantly giving orders. But Jeff works better with limits and attention. I think he needs more rules and steering than I like to use. I was much more independent in my play according to my mother, which makes me want to allow the kids to play together, and by themselves without standing over them. I have learned to think of more structured guidelines when working with Jeff than with others. Instead of letting him go anywhere in the room to read, he has a spot that I ask him to sit in. Rather than totally open free play, I try to steer him toward a specific area. When he lacks this type of structure that the others prefer to do without, he has a difficult time controlling his behavior.

Jeff doesn't seem to have much control over his actions outside of what goes on with a teacher. Six is young to expect him to follow directions because he "should," but I'm concerned about allowing his tantrums or misbehavior to dictate how much time I can spend with other children.

Jeff is a wonderful boy to work with because he is interested and energetic. While he is more than willing to say when he "hates" something, he is also more excited by fun activities than the others. The problem is that Jeff is very time-consuming. Every time I give a direction or ask him to do something, I know he's not going to follow it so that I have to repeat myself. I also find that at times when he's doing well and I move on to another child, he starts doing little things that he shouldn't. It's tough to balance out when I should go back to him instead of the other kids and when I should tell him to stop but continue what I am doing.

It seems that all the volunteers at the camp have their favorites, mine being Jeff, and so we pay more attention to that student. But because I'm not there in the role of Big Brother or Big Sister like the other volunteers, I have other things to do. Jeff doesn't have a big brother so I think it is good for me to spend extra time with him working and playing. Over the next few weeks I am going to spend time with him when I can and encourage him. When Holly needs me to do something else or another child needs help, I am going to explain to Jeff that I like working with him but he needs to help me out and continue his task while I go somewhere else. I will come back and see how he's doing as soon as I can; he should wait patiently.

That's a mouthful but I think it's understandable to a 6-year-old although it may not be what he wants. I explain that I will do what I need to and come back to him as soon as I can without neglecting another task or child.

There are several reasons I haven't done this before. It feels good to have Jeff want me working with him and no one else. It feels like an accomplishment when he is acting up and I am able to get him back on track. He is also more enjoyable to work with than some of the other kids even when he misbehaves. We play some fun games together and I think I work with him to avoid other difficult children or tasks. The last reason that I have put this off is because it is easier to do what he wants than to deal with his misbehavior.

I only work with Jeff two of the five afternoons he spends at the camp, so I would be interested to find out if he has the same behavior with different volunteers on the other days. If I find a similar situation, we could talk about what others did to lessen his response or decide to use the plan I stated earlier. I'm not sure that wanting my time is a problem. Children love when adults pay attention to them, but I worry about Jeff's using misbehavior to gain attention.

I think it is important that he doesn't learn to gain attention by any means necessary, especially if it means inappropriate behavior. I also worry that my focus with Jeff distances the other children from me. I miss out on what I could learn from working with them and also what I could offer them.

Log for Friday April 3—Jill Berkowitz

Sequence of Events
- Arrived at Smithfield Elementary at 2:00 P.M.
- Went around talking and playing with different groups of children
- Had snack
- Took group of children outside
- Went home

Description of a Specific Episode.   At 2:30, I brought about ten children ranging from kindergarten to fourth grade outside. One girl in particular, Rebecca (who, at 6 years old, was in first grade), asked me to come and push her on the swings.

After a minute or two of pushing Rebecca, I realized that she wasn't doing anything to keep herself going, so I said, "Rebecca, do you know how to pump?"

"Not really," she answered me.

"OK, well, why don't I try to teach you now?" I asked her. "Ya!" Rebecca answered excitedly. "All right! Now there's only two things you need to do to pump," I told her, "you only need to bend your legs, and then straighten them. You can try to bend them on your way down, and straighten them on your way up. Ready to try?" I asked.

Rebecca started bending and straightening her legs in quick, choppy movements, only moving back and forth a few inches or so.

"You almost have it!" I told her. "Just try to keep your legs straight for a little longer before you bend them. . . ." I said as she continued scissoring her legs back and forth.

"You know what?" I told her. "Why don't I get on the swing next to you and show you how I do it and then we can swing together?"

"OK!" Rebecca answered.

So I got on the swing next to Rebecca and started pumping, showing her how her legs should be, when to straighten them and when to bend them.

"Great job, Rebecca!" I said. "See how we're going higher now? Now just remember to straighten . . . bend . . . straighten . . . bend. . . ." I repeated the words with the corresponding actions as we did them. After a few minutes of watching me pump and doing exactly what I was doing, Rebecca began to look away and pump on her own, straightening and bending her legs at exactly the right moments so that she was swinging higher and higher.

"I'm doing it!" she called out, a big smile on her face.

"Yep, you're doing it *perfectly!*" I replied as she continued going up and down.

Analysis.   After a minute or so of pushing Rebecca on the swing, it occurred to me that she may not know how to pump, and if she relied forever on people pushing her, she'd never learn how to swing by herself! So I asked Rebecca if she knew how to pump, and when she answered no I asked if she wanted to learn how. I asked Rebecca if she wanted to learn how to pump rather than simply telling her how to do it because I wanted Rebecca to be the one making up her mind to learn. I think that when children are allowed to take the initiative and decide themselves to learn that the learning process goes much more quickly and easily. When children feel they are forced to learn (e.g., "You have to learn how to pump, or you'll never be able to swing by yourself. This is how to do it.") they may feel some pressure if they don't grasp what to do, and they also will be less interested in learning when they feel it is imposed on them. I know that in many teaching/learning situations the teacher has no choice but to present certain information the learner is "required" to know, but when presented in a nonconfrontational, more give-and-take manner, students may be more willing and interested in learning.

Fortunately for me, in this situation Rebecca was very willing to learn, and the first thing I did was to explain to her what to do with her legs. I considered describing to Rebecca why her legs had to bend and straighten in order to make her move (such as by saying that the bending pushes the air back and that the straightening pushes the air forward, or something along those lines) but I thought that those concepts might be a little much for a 6-year-old to grasp—it was enough for her to remember what to do with her legs.

When I saw that Rebecca was still having trouble applying what I was *saying* to what she was *doing*, I decided actually to show her how to pump. Many students learn differently—some pick up better on aural information, while some need visuals in order to make a concept truly clear. Rebecca seemed to need some visual cues (as do I!)—once she saw me pumping right next to her she was able to mimic my movements and feel what pumping felt like. I combined visual and audio methods of teaching (both by showing Rebecca how to pump and by reciting what we were doing as we did it— "pump, straighten, pump, straighten," etc.) to try to ingrain in Rebecca what she was doing to pump as she was doing it. Once Rebecca felt how to pump, she was able to stop relying on me and to pump based on what she had learned.

I think this "lesson" went well and I was really pleased that I was able to teach Rebecca how to pump. I was able to apply what I knew, using audio and visual enforcers, to increase a child's knowledge and self-confidence. I realize that this is a very simple concept and isn't too important in life, but to a 6-year-old child it means a lot to be able to swing by herself. When I saw how happy Rebecca was when she was finally able to pump on her own, I had such a great sense of accomplishment, and I felt like a real teacher.

Sample Progress Reports

I Think I Can, I Think I Can

ERIC PANNESE

Every Tuesday I awoke early in the morning, hours before any college student opens his eyes, to make my way over to Eastern Heights Elementary School. Once there, I worked as an assistant to Ms. Joyce in a classroom of 20 third graders. The students worked on mathematics, a subject I am comfortable with, during my two hours in the classroom. My duties consisted of locating and helping those children who were having difficulty with their work. Frequently, I would take a child to a table in the back of the room and tutor him or her in a one-on-one setting. Other times I would work with a group of children all having difficulty with the same assignment. No two learning situations were ever alike, which made me realize the wide variety of learners that exist in a classroom.

Prior to beginning my fieldwork, I formulated several goals and concerns for my students and myself. However, when outlining my goals and concerns I had assumed that I would be working at the local correctional facility. Perhaps what is most interesting is that almost all of my goals and concerns, with the exception of those regarding my personal safety, extended into my teaching experience at Eastern Heights Elementary School. More relevant is my microgoals paper, because it was written at a time when I had been working at Eastern Heights. This paper will first touch on the goals and concerns of both compositions, examining how successful I was in accomplishing my goals and overcoming my concerns. Second, this paper will provide an in-depth analysis of the role that confidence plays in a learning situation.

My Goals and Concerns paper surprises me because of the relevancy of the concepts, even though it was written for a different learning situation. What this tells me is that my goals and concerns were more generally related to teaching rather than to the situation in which I was placed. For example, I worried that I would not be able to teach my learners effectively. This concern is relevant at the correctional center, Eastern Heights Elementary School, or in virtually any learning situation. Not surprisingly, I did come across this problem quite frequently in my fieldwork, as some of my students did not always understand my guidance. As expected, this was a very difficult concern to deal with; however, I learned how to alleviate it using different procedures. One method I found to be very effective was to break a problem down into smaller parts. This often included asking several questions to guide my learner toward the answer. Log #2, page 12, provides an example of this procedure as I helped Lisa find nouns and verbs in various sentences. Instead of just plowing right into the material, I stopped and asked her if she knew what a noun was. Once I got her mind thinking about nouns, she was able to spot them more easily. Interestingly, this thought process did not transfer over directly to verbs. I had to prompt her ten minutes later asking for the definition of a verb and we worked from there.

Word problems are not the only type of examples that can be broken down to better facilitate learning. Math questions readily lend themselves to such analysis. In Log #7, page 19, I worked with Stephen on division. Although he had blocks to assist him in solving the problem, he was not making proper use of them. Immediately, I broke into a series of questions prompting him to take out the correct number of blocks and then break them down into smaller groups to solve the question. I found it much easier to divide the problem into several segments in this episode compared to that of Log #2. At the time of Log #7, I had worked with the students for five additional weeks and had gained confidence over that time. I did not hesitate to attack the problem right away and I feel this was a noticeable improvement in my teaching skills.

Another useful mechanism in helping a student who is having difficulty is to take a step back from the problem and attack it using a different angle. I tried this in Log #10, page 25, with Alissa who was puzzled by the most recent lesson involving fractions. Realizing that she might be more of a visual learner, I told her to put her pencil down so that we could work with plastic shapes instead of the numbers on the page. Much to my delight, this approach worked magnificently as she played with the shapes and derived solutions to the questions. My error in this situation was that I relied on the shapes and did not work with the problem outside of the visual aids. As I stated in my analysis of that log, perhaps I would make an attempt to wean Alissa away from the shapes and toward solving the problem numerically.

Improving my teaching skills was very important to me as I embarked on a semester of fieldwork. As the saying goes, "practice makes perfect," and I was confident that I would be able to develop teaching abilities as I spent time in a classroom every week. My development came about in a myriad of different ways. In the examples previously mentioned, I was able to recognize when a problem must be broken down to enhance a student's understanding. Not only was I able to make this recognition, I was also able to divide the problems more effectively as I became more experienced.

Another area in which I developed over the course of my tenure was in disciplining the students. Initially, I was worried about how to handle a student presenting a behavior problem. Over time, I learned how to handle the students through watching Ms. Joyce and soon I was able to discipline effectively when necessary. One of my logs, Log #6, page 16, focused entirely on an episode I had while bringing all 20 students to gym class. I struggled to maintain control as they broke into a race down the hall before I knew what had just passed me! Stopping the line and threatening the students with a trip back to their classroom proved to be a successful conclusion to this discipline situation.

Turning to my Goals paper, the central theme focused on having a positive impact on one or more of the children. I'm not sure I'm happy with the extent to which I was able to accomplish this goal. Given the structure of the learning environment and the time frame in which I was working, I did not have much of an opportunity to socialize with my students. There were occasions when they would ask me about Cornell and college life in general, and I would tell them how much I loved it. I attempted to instill a desire in my learners to go to college. I told them how it was important that they work extremely hard throughout their schooling so that they can one day go to a top university. Outside of this, however, I do not really feel as though I had a personal effect on any of my learners. Perhaps, this is because I was only in class once a week. It may also have been due to the fact that I was working with third graders. When I think about my secondary educational career as a student, I know that I did not develop personal relationships with my teachers until high school. My expectation was probably derived from the fact that I look back at my relationships with my teachers with great fondness. I probably should not have expected the same from third graders and this is a goal that I would change for future situations involving younger students.

Another microgoal that rapidly became a recurring theme in my logs was related to confidence. When writing my Goals paper, I wrote that I wanted to help my third graders gain self-assuredness. Although my reflections at the beginning of the semester did not touch very often on the subject, it quickly became a central issue in my final logs. In Log #9, page 22, I wrote that individuals are easily discouraged or frustrated when trying to learn new, difficult material. It does not matter whether you are a third-grader striving to understand fractions or a college student attempting to understand linear algebra, we all face challenges. Conquering these obstacles then becomes the focus of the teacher and learner together.

Confidence is central to any learning situation, but rising to the occasion can be extremely difficult at times. It is always easier just to say "I can't do it," as I talked about in Log #10. However, learners will not be as tempted to forfeit a problem if they have strong confidence on their abilities. Confidence comes from many different sources, including one's personality. Some people are natural "go-getters"; they have a drive for success within them. Other people derive confidence from success. Without a doubt there are a multitude of sources that contribute to one's overall conviction.

Writing about confidence has caused me to take a step back and look at myself as I approach final exam period here at Cornell. The mere thought of my final examination in Economics 331, Money and Credit, causes me to shudder. Why? Because I am not comfortable with the material. I have spent over 40 hours in the last three days studying the information and even though I may know it very well, I am terrified of the exam. When I enter an exam with such trepidation, I generally fail to answer all of the questions to the best of my ability. I am not comfortable enough to relax and answer the exam properly. In thinking about my other economics class, Econ 341, Labor Economics, I realize that I hardly study for this class. One reason I am able to succeed without countless hours of work is that I am confident I will do well. Much of this confidence is derived from the fact that I have done well with similar material in the past. In Economics 331, I had studied diligently for days before the midterm and I only got a B–. Given this experience I feel as though I am not capable of doing any better on the final exam.

The best way to overcome a lack of confidence is to succeed; however, success does not always come easily. Past experiences can play a major role in determining future success. I see this as a student at Cornell and as a teacher at Eastern Heights. One advantage that I currently possess as a teacher is that I am a student at the same time. I am able to build from my personal experiences to prevent my learners from falling into a trap of frustration. I believe that the factors most detrimental to my confidence are past failures; more significantly, past failures in which I gave my best effort. It is one thing to fail an exam without studying for it, but to fail after studying for 40 hours leaves a deep wound. Although third graders aren't dealing with prelims and finals yet, they do have to deal with failure. It can be tough for one student to be sitting at his desk struggling desperately to complete his worksheet only to see the girl at the desk across from him breeze through it in ten seconds. I find as a teacher that it is important to make sure that students don't feel upset if they are not the fastest learners in the class. One mistake teachers often make is to reward the first person finished with an assignment. I disagree with this tactic as it punishes slow learners and compensates fast learners. The pace at which someone learns new material is not the most important aspect of learning, but rather how well someone understands the information is much more critical.

When working one-on-one with a student, there are many ways to build confidence. I have found the most obvious technique, positive comments, to be the most effective. Third graders love to hear that they're doing well. Looking at the episode section of Logs #2 and #7, I made extensive use of positive reinforcement; for example, comments such as "great job" and "that's right." My inclusion of positive reinforcement grew as the semester progressed and I saw how well the students responded to my comments. Underlying my positive reinforcement was a basis for building up confidence. In working with individuals I was able to tell them regularly how well they were doing. As the saying goes, "If you hear something enough times, you have to start believing it at some point." I believe that my repetitive affirmations to my learners helped build their confidence because they gradually came to believe that they could accomplish the given task.

Preventing failure is also a key component to maintaining conviction. Not to say that all teachers want their students to fail, but there are the select few who seem not to care about their students. For example, here at Cornell economics classes are often scaled to a B–. However, I have had professors who scaled the mean to a C+. What is their motivation to give out such harsh grades? Perhaps they want to be feared by future students or at least have a reputation as being difficult. Regardless of their motivation, I feel the premise is immoral. I feel that teachers or professors should want their students to do well. This thought process can be transferred to my third-grade classroom in that the focus should be student-oriented. This focus is directly related to confidence as discussed earlier in this paper. It can be difficult to rebound from a failure; thus, if teachers have the capacity to prevent such an occurrence, they should do everything in their power to do so. Success, not failure, breeds success.

February seems like a long time ago, yet it was only ten weeks ago. In those short ten weeks I began and completed my fieldwork in a third-grade classroom. Ten weeks ago I had goals. Today I have reflections relating to my goals. Fortunately, the central theme of my logs, confidence, coincided with one of my goals stated earlier in the semester. I had hoped to be able to instill a sense of conviction in the students I worked with. Having completed my classroom experience, I feel as though I successfully fostered confidence within my learners.

I feel fortunate that the common theme of my logs corresponded with one of my initial goals. Just as learners have to strive to achieve their goals, I also had to over-come fears as I attempted to fulfill my goals as a teacher. I did not enter the classroom with the same level of confidence that I departed with. My assurance grew as time passed because I was having great success with my learners. Therefore, my accom-plishments as a teacher reinforced my confidence in my abilities.

I found self-assurance valuable in teaching the children as well as in disciplining them. When I first arrived at the school I did not have the authority or the ability to enforce discipline. As I grew more comfortable in my role, however, I slowly devel-oped the required skills to control the class. On more than one occasion, after having been there several weeks, I was left alone with the class because Ms. Joyce knew that I could handle the situation.

The similarity in concerns and issues related to teachers and learners is much closer than I would have anticipated at the outset of the semester. Quite simply, I never realized what it takes to teach. Having been a student all my life, I feel I have a good understanding of how students think, including what motivates and prevents them from doing well. Little did I know that the same element plays a determining role in the lives of teachers as well. That element? Self-confidence.

Questioning My Identity and Challenging My Perspectives on Diversity

Masako Iwata

Mrs. Danato's first-grade classroom at Susan B. Anthony Elementary School was unfa-miliar territory for me; and deep down inside, a sense of fear crawled up and poked its face out at me. I didn't want to see fear's whole identity nor did I want even to admit its existence. But in the classroom where I had no choice but to take the "students on," my fear revealed itself all too clearly to me as I was busy frantically trying to see what tricks I had in my pocket.

This fear questioned who I was, and moreover, brought this side by side with the notion of who I believed I was. It forced me to examine how my identity as an Asian American female influenced me to be a certain type of teacher. It also chal-lenged me to go outside the safe bounds and limits I set up for myself according to the demands and needs of the students. My experience with more ethnically and socioeconomically diverse groups of students in this first-grade classroom really challenged my whole perspective on diversity. I learned that my understanding and tolerance for diversity was not as perfect as I prided myself on. My experience with Mrs. Danato and her first-grade classroom broadened my life experience and taught me what it takes to be a good teacher in a society of people from different unique backgrounds and experiences.

My first day of class was full of surprises. The class was extremely disorganized and the students had bad behavior problems. I was equally surprised, somewhat dis-turbed, by how the teacher, Mrs. Danato, was handling the class. She was very strict and stern with them and was, in my opinion at the time, very scary and mean. But she had warned me beforehand that I would be surprised at how she handled the class-room. She also informed me that the students with the worst behavior problems in the class were Malika, Jeanne, and Michael. Because Mrs. Danato told me they had prob-lems beforehand, I felt I already had a bias toward them. Also, I have to admit, with honesty, that I was a bit nervous about how to interact with these children because they were African American and I was Asian American. This was the first confronta-tion with my biases and preconceived notions about the children. I was equally con-cerned about how they viewed me, an Asian female with a foreign name. I did not know how to respond when the children started repeating my name with a strange voice when I introduced myself to them. I feared that because I was Asian American as well as not as outspoken as others might be, I would be invisible. I feared they would not listen to my demands and instructions.

From the first day of class, the students forced me to take on the teaching role I was there for, whether I was comfortable with it or not. This meant understanding the dynamics of the classroom and the students in it. Though the classroom was familiar to me, I felt very confused and nervous about what was new to me. I think memories of fear and shyness that were so prevalent during my childhood experiences at school came back to haunt me. I knew too well what it felt like to be singled out because of color or ethnicity. The unfamiliar aspects were the fact that now I could no longer be shy, stay in the back, and not be seen. I was a teacher, or at the least, an adult to these children, and I could not retreat to my own world in which I only perceived things that I chose to see. As an adult, I saw children with different abilities, socioeconomic backgrounds, cultures, race, etc. But seeing things in perspective now, I know that I saw some children through the glasses of bias and discrimination. That is, from the very beginning, I judged and labeled certain children as being a certain way. I did so because I was inexperienced and everything was new to me; I was trying to understand as fast as possible how to interact and deal with these children.

My reflection in my very first log reveals, rather shamefully, my biased perspective. I wrote about Michael, "who can't read nor speak a full sentence without it being choppy, seemed like a very warm, affectionate child but didn't have the skills to do the things I demanded of him." This was my first encounter with Michael and I "sensed that his judgment skills weren't like an average child's." Though I now know that all children do not naturally have these skills, back then, I thought that Michael was one of the few that still "couldn't get it." I viewed Michael, an African American boy who was not verbally articulate and who disobeyed me, as someone who was different. Therefore, I might not be able to communicate with him as I could with others. This bias could have influenced my attitude toward him, especially with my motivation for teaching him. Somewhere in the back of my mind this bias could have led me to believe that I couldn't help him because he was "different."

The children in the class who were having the most difficult time, both academically and behaviorally, were all African American. Although I believed myself to be racially aware because I was a female of color myself, I saw myself generalizing the African American race as more inclined toward trouble. Additionally, I found myself having a negative or indifferent attitude toward them more than the other children. Curiously, I found that I had more pictures of the children I considered to be the "cutest." I clearly had my "favorites" and "not-so-favorites." I wondered why Kimberly, who Mrs. Danato said came from an affectionate and supportive family, had a short attention span, among other problems, and was behind other students in her academic levels. I saw how Malika had real behavior and disciplinary problems, and I thought it may have stemmed from his mother being so young still. I also wondered why Michael, whose dad was a pastor, swore in class and purposely disrespected me.

I realized that I've done exactly the same thing to another race that upsets me when others generalize about my Asian race, and I was deeply humbled. This humbling experience opened my eyes to areas in my thinking that I really needed to work on to change. It also taught me to be more tolerant toward others who may do the same but do not realize what they are doing by stereotyping a certain race to be a certain way. I felt fortunate to be able to identify and start an effort to change my biases. On the other hand, most of the time, children cannot identify what their biases are. There were many times during the semester when I heard children verbally hurting others on purpose. Many of the African American children were calling each other ugly and stupid. African American girls were more often made fun of in how they looked. I was deeply hurt by the children's words toward each other because I knew that their words had come directly from what society tells them about what ugly and pretty are. Women of color, African Americans especially, are branded as physically unattractive and worthless. Even more, I observed that children knew what would hurt each other the most. Through these experiences, the leader in me was challenged and the teacher within me was called on.

But another insight I learned was that I could not completely disregard their background and race. All these children came from diverse backgrounds. I needed to be aware and understand this to be able to better meet their needs and wants. I recognized this somewhat even in the first day when I was dealing with Michael and felt that he might not understand what I was trying to tell him, because of our unfamiliarity with each other. Malika came from a family where he was the oldest and was raised by his grandmother because his teenage mother could not handle the children. I have to keep this in mind in order to be able to understand why he has a behavior problem and has a hard time following directions. It was obvious to me that he was not doing it on purpose to stir up the teacher's temper, but rather he did not understand the concept of discipline because of the lack of it in his life outside of school. Many students, such as Ilana and Ahmad, are ESL students and may not understand everything that people tell them in English. These are only a few of the deeper insights into understanding each child as an individual who brings his or her past and personality to school.

As the semester progressed, the diversity issue hit me even harder. Rather than the issue of race that I confronted in the beginning, I now dealt with the realization that all the children in the classroom had different learning needs. In truth, they actually stemmed from common human needs such as affection and acceptance. For instance, I learned that Jeanne needed instructions to be presented in a more step-by-step manner and needed praise for working hard every step of the way. Kimberly, who was aware that her own reading and writing skills were not as developed as others in the class, didn't want to be treated or given a different assignment than others. Malika, who got sent to the principal quite often because of behavior problems, persistently called for attention from the teacher to inform him that he was doing the right thing. He loved the attention and praise just as any other child. They all, in their own ways, informed me of who they are, what they need, and how they need it.

Looking back before my fieldwork experience, I thought most children learned their "life skills" such as respect, patience, and empathy toward others through observation and time. I overgeneralized my experience, one heavily influenced by my own culture and upbringing, as one common among others. I had limited experience with how people grew up, and I could not envision growing up without knowing these life skills. But now, after seeing so many different children, I realized that these skills don't come naturally; they are learned. I saw that one of the main responsibilities of the teacher is to make sure the students have and can use these life skills.

Not only did my experience teach me about the diversity among the students in the classroom, it also taught me of my own diversity and how it influenced my teaching style. I had a lot of difficulty with learning and using some specific words that some teachers here in the United States use, both because I was a novice teacher and because I was raised in a traditional Japanese family. I noticed how the teachers would phrase questions and comments ending with names such as "honey" or "darling" that added that extra effect of showing the teacher's affection toward the children. I did not and could not use this extra vocabulary because it just seemed so unnatural to me. But at the same time, I felt as though I needed to use this type of language.

Furthermore, because of my personality and my culture, I maintained a more calm, patient, observant nature, rather than an authoritarian, action-oriented one.

I never questioned or undermined the supervising teacher's position with the students. In my statement of goals for learners, I wrote, "I will not be the strict enforcer of the rules and punishments, as Mrs. Danato prefers, because it is better for the students to have one main authority figure that has consistent guidelines and predictable responses." This created a big problem when I was dealing with the children alone and I saw a lot of unacceptable behavior. First of all, I did not know what to do and how to enforce what was right. Second, I felt as though I did not have the power or authority to be able to take the necessary action. Many times, "I felt frustrated and out of control of the situation when the children would not listen to me and follow my directions. . . . [it] showed that I do not present myself as a person of authority or threat." My inaction and lack of strictness was due to the interplay of the limits from my cultural background and the limits of what role I was expected to play in the classroom. I simply observed how the supervising teacher dealt with the children. Few times did I actually get directly involved with the students and the problem itself.

Every day, there was some type of conflict in the classroom. My culture had taught me to be patient, never to raise my voice, and that anger was a sign of weakness. Mainly for this reason, "I have never, ever lost my temper and raised my voice" toward the children. Even when I consciously made a decision to be stern, which was only when I felt that it was absolutely necessary, I was cautious not to sound judgmental and mean. But as I wrote in one of my logs, there were times when I thought that "maybe I needed to get upset . . . and raise my voice to communicate to the students that their behavior was not acceptable. But I simply couldn't, didn't know how to. I was afraid of what might happen. I was afraid of how they might react." When the supervising teacher raised her voice, I shuddered in surprise and gazed at how she handled the situation.

I also realized that even if I could raise my voice and be strict, I didn't know if it was my position to do so or not. "I felt powerless because I felt that I did not have the authority to punish or enforce some disciplinary action on any one of them." Viewing the situation in perspective, because I was not expected to discipline the students and was not personally responsible for disciplining them, I did not. I was clearly aware of my position from the beginning when I established my goals and concerns.

But reflecting back on the logs, I can see that I've learned a lot and have made definite progress in being more stern. I was challenged to go outside the boundaries of what I was familiar and comfortable with. My fear in the beginning was due to these children questioning my identity and my culture. I felt as though my personality did not fit into the method of teaching in the United States. I felt as though I needed to conform completely to how I observed other teachers, direct class. But in the end, they actually strengthened my identity and culture. I can keep my culture but need to alter my actions according to what the students' needs are. I know that there is a need for discipline in all cultures, but the mode of addressing what is right and wrong may be different. As a teacher, I need to be flexible and match the various learning styles of the students. I need to go beyond the walls of my experience and try to understand the experiences of my students. By doing so, my perspective on diversity and life will broaden and then maybe I will have the background to be a good teacher.

In the beginning when the students would not listen to me, I just simply did not know what to do. I was really afraid of hurting their feelings by raising my voice or disciplining them. In my logs, I do not really state what direct methods I can use to solve problems. But now, I have better skills to tackle the issues. I've made some progress on the issue of being strict and stern. I know that there is a time and place to be strict and show that I am upset at the students. It is necessary at times and it is my responsibility to teach them what is good and what is bad behavior. I would be doing them a disservice by not doing anything; that would be enforcing their actions—it would be like telling them in one episode that "it was okay to use verbal name calling and physical violence to resolve conflict."

My experience at Susan B. Anthony opened my eyes to the issue of diversity by questioning and challenging my beliefs, which I discovered to be deeply biased. My bias toward certain students affected how I interacted with and viewed them. My bias about myself and who I believed I was caused me to react to situations in ways that I was either familiar or comfortable with. I realized that with all my biases, I needed to go beyond the confined boundaries I had set around me. As a teacher, I was responsible and obligated to my students to be able to see each as an individual with different needs and backgrounds and to be able to adjust my approach and teaching style according to them.

Names of people, places, and schools have been changed in order to protect the privacy of those involved.

ADDITIONAL BIBLIOGRAPHY

Belenky, M. F., B. M. Clinchy, et al. (1986). *A woman's way of knowing: The development of self, voice and mind.* New York: Basic Books.

Carter, R. (1998). *Mapping the mind.* London: Weildenfeld and Nicholson.

Family Life Development Center. (2002). *Depositing data with the national data archive on child abuse and neglect.* Ithaca, NY: Cornell University.

Cuban, L. (2001). *Oversold and underused: Computers in the classroom.* Cambridge, MA: Harvard University Press.

Fillmore, L. W., and L. M. Meyer, eds. (1992). *The curriculum and linguistic minorities. Handbook on research on curriculum.* New York: Macmillan.

Garbarino, J. (1995). *Raising children in a socially toxic environment.* San Francisco: Jossey-Bass.

Gardner, H. (1999). *The disciplined mind.* New York: Simon & Schuster.

Hale, J. (1982). *Black children: Their roots, culture, and learning styles.* Provo, UT: Brigham Young Press.

Holt, J. (1995). *How children fail.* Reading, MA: Merloyd Lawrence.

Horn, E., et al., eds. (2002). *Classroom models of individualized instruction. Widening the circle: Including children with disabilities in preschool programs.* New York: Teacher's College Press.

John-Steiner, V., et al., eds. (1972). *Styles of learning: Styles of teaching.* The function of language in the classroom. New York: Teacher's College Press.

Kronick, R. F. (1997). *At risk youth: Theory practice, reform.* New York: Garland.

Levine, M. (2002). *A mind at a time.* New York: Simon & Schuster.

National Center for Educational Statistics. (2002). *Internet access in U.S. public schools and classrooms: 1994–2001.* Retrieved December 11, 2002, from nces.ed.gov/pubs2002/internet/.

Nerney, M. (1998). *What can we do to protect our youth from drugs and alcohol?* Ithaca, NY: Cornell University Press.

Perry, I. (1988). "A black student's reflection on private and public schools." *Harvard Educational Review* 58:332–336.

Ravitch, D., and J. P. Viteritti, eds. (2003). *Kids stuff: Marketing sex and violence to America's children.* Baltimore, MD: The John Hopkins University Press.

Rhoded, J., et al. (1999). "The influence of mentoring on the peer relationships of foster youth in relative and non-relative care." *Journal of Research on Adolescents* 9(2):185–201.

Scales, P. C. (1996). "A responsive ecology for positive young adolescent development." *The Clearing House* 69(4):226.

Scales, P. C., et al. (2000). "Contribution of developmental assets to the prediction of thriving among adolescents." *Applied Developmental Science* 4(1):27–46.

Stepp, L. S. (2000). *Our last best shot: Guiding our children through early adolescence.* New York: Riverhead Books.

Werner, E. E., and Smith, R. S. (1977). *Kauai's children come of age.* Honolulu: University of Hawaii Press.

Index

INDEX